You'll be Sor-ree!

YOU'LL BE SOR-REE!

A GUADALCANAL MARINE
REMEMBERS THE PACIFIC WAR

Sid Phillips

BERKLEY CALIBER, NEW YORK

BERKLEY BOOKS
Published by the Penguin Group
Penguin Group (USA) Inc.
375 Hudson Street, New York, New York 10014, USA
Penguin Group (Canada), 90 Eglinton Avenue East, Suite 700, Toronto, Ontario M4P 2Y3, Canada
(a division of Pearson Penguin Canada Inc.) • Penguin Books Ltd., 80 Strand, London WC2R 0RL,
England • Penguin Group Ireland, 25 St. Stephen's Green, Dublin 2, Ireland (a division of Penguin
Books Ltd.) • Penguin Group (Australia), 250 Camberwell Road, Camberwell, Victoria 3124, Australia
(a division of Pearson Australia Group Pty. Ltd.) • Penguin Books India Pvt. Ltd., 11 Community
Centre, Panchsheel Park, New Delhi—110 017, India • Penguin Group (NZ), 67 Apollo Drive,
Rosedale, Auckland 0632, New Zealand (a division of Pearson New Zealand Ltd.) • Penguin Books
(South Africa) (Pty.) Ltd., 24 Sturdee Avenue, Rosebank, Johannesburg 2196, South Africa

Penguin Books Ltd., Registered Offices: 80 Strand, London WC2R 0RL, England

The publisher does not have any control over and does not assume any responsibility
for author or third-party websites or their content.

YOU'LL BE SOR-REE!

PUBLISHING HISTORY
Valor Studios hardcover edition / February 2010
Berkey Caliber trade paperback edition / April 2012

ISBN: 978-0-425-24629-0

PRINTED IN THE UNITED STATES OF AMERICA

10 9 8 7 6 5 4 3 2 1

Penguin is committed to publishing works of quality and integrity.
In that spirit, we are proud to offer this book to our readers,
however, the story, the experiences, and the words
are the author's alone.

ALWAYS LEARNING   PEARSON

To my wonderful family, who
pushed me to write this in the first place.

Preface

I began writing *You'll Be Sor-ree!* in the year of our Lord 1997, when I was seventy-three years old. As time advanced and I grew a little older and older, my family repeatedly asked me to write down some of my experiences of historical interest concerning World War II. So, I did. When I completed my memoirs in 1998, I printed them in a loosely bound fashion and distributed them to my family. They were received with such astounding enthusiasm that I had to have more copies printed, then more, then more. With each print run, I added new material, corrections, and improvements that have led to the publication of this book.

Since there are many scholarly works and excellent books already in print concerning World War II, I have chosen to simply recall certain events that happened to me, with special emphasis on the humorous ones. In other words, there will be no attempt to compete with all of the good books about the war that are already in existence and there will be little effort to focus on strategy and the big picture.

Any old Marine will quickly recognize this as a collection of "sea stories." Therefore, all you have, Dear Reader, is my promise that these pages will be without fictional embellishment insofar as my ancient memory can recall them. This will, most of all, be my effort to show that American humor and nonsense, as much as patriotism and courage, were of vital importance to lift our nation through those dark hours and days of World War II.

Dr. Sidney C. Phillips
Mobile, Alabama

YOU'LL BE SOR-REE!

1

W.O. continued to wipe the marble top of the soda fountain in his perpetual way, and then said, "Sid, let's go join the Navy in the morning."

===

Because of the principle of cause and effect, everything must have a beginning, so I shall choose December 7, 1941. Any American old enough to remember can tell you exactly what he or she was doing that day when he or she first heard the news of the bombing of Pearl Harbor. The only exception to that statement that I know of is my wife, Mary, who said she could not remember exactly what she was doing on December 7, 1941, but was probably, "Just thinking about boys as usual."

Should I tell you immediately what I was doing or should I first tell you that those were very dark, almost black days for our nation? War was raging in Europe and, thanks to the English Channel and the RAF, Great Britain alone remained unconquered in Europe against the Axis powers (Germany and Italy) and Hitler was winning the Battle of the Atlantic with his submarine navy. America was poorly prepared for war and our pitifully under-strength armed forces had obsolete weapons in all branches with, perhaps, our Navy being a little more modern than our Army. Japan was officially neutral in the European conflict, although she had been at war in China for years and, thus, was industrially geared for war. Russia, as I recall, at that moment in time, seemed to be a very remote and uncertain factor, a known surplus of men with very little else to stop the onslaught of Hitler.

When the attack commenced at Pearl Harbor at 7 a.m. on that fateful Sunday morning, it was 2 p.m. in Mobile, Alabama. We began to get the news of the attack on Sunday afternoon, just minutes after the attack began. I was sitting on a white enameled soda fountain stool in the Albright & Wood drugstore at the corner of Dauphin and Ann streets, drinking a vanilla milkshake and rotating the stool with my body motion, when some lady burst through the side door and screamed

"Turn on the radio!" It is strange how I can remember the floor was of white and black ceramic tiles, each tile about a foot square, arranged in checkerboard design. I had paid a whole nickel for the milkshake that contained three scoops of ice cream instead of the one that it was supposed to, which my good friend W.O. Brown had prepared. W.O. was one of my closest friends and, though still in Murphy High School, worked as a soda jerk whenever he could to make money to help in his very large family. I had finished Murphy High School six months earlier in June 1941, and had a good job downtown in the First National Bank building with the U.S. Engineers as a "runner" carrying maps between departments. It paid $90 a month, which I was saving to maybe start at Auburn the next year, taking goodness knows what, but getting precious college credits that my parents were constantly reminding my sister and me that we must have. Going to college was understood as the next step in life in our family. Not going was not even an option. Ninety dollars a month was a very good salary for a boy just out of high school in 1941.

The radio announcers were talking about Pearl Harbor on every station and it seemed I was the only person in the drugstore who knew the location of Pearl Harbor. My two uncles were in the regular Navy and Uncle Joe Tucker had been stationed in Pearl Harbor, so I was familiar with the name and could show off by telling the crowd it was in Hawaii. Hawaii in those days seemed about as close as Mars today. The news was not very specific as to the extent of damage, but it became clear the Japanese effort was of major proportion and this could only mean we were in the war. All faces were very grave and nobody said very much. I do recall some ladies started to cry as the radio announcer told us the casualties were in the thousands. W.O. continued to wipe the marble top of the soda fountain in his perpetual way, and then said, "Sid, let's go join the Navy in the morning." My response was "OK," and I left on my bicycle to go home and be with my family. I recall the sky was clear and the afternoon sunshine very bright as I rode out Brown Street to my home in Monterey Place.

I had turned seventeen in September 1941, and didn't yet have a driver's license. Actually, my parents did not want my sister or me to risk wrecking the precious car. Naturally, the family was already aware of the attack and filled with deep concern when I arrived and we all stayed glued to the radio as the same news was repeated over and over without much more clarification of specifics or details of the actual damage.

The next morning I met W.O. downtown at the fountain in the center of Bienville Square as we had planned, and we walked over to the Federal Building. The time was about eight and we planned to be the early birds at the recruiting station. We knew all of the armed forces recruiting stations were located on the first floor of the Federal Building. There was a line two abreast from the door of the Navy recruiting office through the lobby, out the door, down the steps, down St. Joseph Street to the corner, around the corner, and out St. Louis Street for half a block. So we walked to the head of the line just to see what was going on. A Marine recruiting sergeant from the office across the hall from the Navy office approached us (there was no crowd in his office) and asked us if we wanted to kill Japs? When we answered in the affirmative, he told us all we would do in the Navy would be to swab decks, but if we wanted to kill Japs we belonged in the Marine Corps, and he guaranteed us the Marine Corps would put us eyeball to eyeball with the Japs. That was about the only thing he told us that wasn't a lie. We were both seventeen years of age and, thus, barely old enough to enlist. He quickly did some preliminary examination tests on us and found I was slightly deficient in my color perception. He assured us the Navy requirements were the same and added the Marine Corps was part of the Navy, in fact the best part, but said we could not get in the regular Navy anyway because our parents were married (my first introduction to the friendly rivalry between the Navy and the Marine Corps). He felt the color perception requirements would be changed in a few days, and suggested we return the day after Christmas. W.O. seemed to be willing to wait until then, so we left with all the necessary papers to prepare and have signed by our parents.

This started a war between my parents, with my father willing to sign because he knew I would be drafted shortly

5

anyway, but my mother holding out because her only two brothers were already in the Navy and she felt that was enough of a contribution on her part. Finally, my father prevailed, and W.O. and I were scheduled to leave Mobile on December 29, 1941, in a group of perhaps ten Marine recruits bound for Birmingham. There is no truth in the story that my family wept all the way to the railroad station because they were afraid I might miss the train. Our group was in high spirits and had a wonderful time being self-appointed experts on all subjects related to war. I remember we repeatedly sang the new song "Chattanooga Choo Choo" and were about as loud and obnoxious on that train as any group of young men could be.

When we arrived in Birmingham with our small suitcases, we walked to a very bad two-story hotel that the U.S. government had chosen for us to spend the night. It was exactly like something out of an old black-and-white Humphrey Bogart movie complete with a huge vertical sign that blinked on and off right outside our window all night. I remember the sign contained hundreds of ordinary house lightbulbs, many of which were burned out, and simply said HOTEL. There was no actual lobby in the hotel, but just a hall leading up to a counter with a clerk and numbered keys hanging on a board behind him. Our group leader (the eldest) had tickets for meals in a nearby greasy spoon café Uncle Sam had chosen for an awful blue plate special. We sat on the stools at the counter. A second cup of coffee would have cost a nickel. We left no tip.

W.O. and I sort of scorned the meatloaf and green peas that night, to have the memory return to haunt us eight months later. As with all seventeen-year-old young men, we felt we already knew everything there was to know that was worth knowing.

2

We noted anyone casually walking by and not in
ranks or formation would always shout
"YOU'LL BE SOR-REE!"

===========

After our arrival at the rundown "Humphrey Bogart
Hotel" in Birmingham, W.O. and I received our key for the
upstairs front room right by the blinking sign. We entered our
room and noted the creaking wooden floors, the old iron bed
made out of fancy pipe that needed paint, the worn pink bed-
spread, dingy sheets and lumpy mattress, window shades with
no curtains, and the lack of any bathroom except the one for

all at the end of the hall, complete with grimy tub, stained toilet, and rusty, chipped hand basin with speckled mirror, and then decided to take off our one and only sport coats (we had not left a fancy wardrobe at home in 1941). We valued our fifteen-dollar Schwobilt coats, so decided to hang them in the closet. The closet door would not open, so we both grabbed the doorknob and tugged with all our might. The door came open, but proved to be a door into the next room where a "Lady" was sitting on the bed wearing exactly nothing. Her figure wasn't too bad! She began screaming at the top of her lungs, so W.O. and I just very, very slowly closed the door and waited for what we knew would be some kind of volcanic eruption. Sure enough, in a few minutes, a policeman with a drawn nickel-plated .38 caliber revolver in hand and the hotel clerk trailing exploded into the room ready to put us in irons.

We managed to quiet them with our simple explanation about the search for a closet, and were assured there was no closet. In a few minutes, another man came in with a hammer and some nails about four inches long and nailed the door shut. We were too young to go searching for a bar, so we just lay down on that lumpy bed and became intoxicated by that flashing sign on the shades. There were no curtains. We wondered if things would get worse. They did.

We were up early the next morning and our Mobile group walked to the nearby Birmingham Marine recruiting office and were sworn into the Marine Corps by an older captain wearing blues with a Sam Brown–type of belt. Other Alabama recruits were there also and we took an ominous oath in a crowded room that let us know in this war for freedom we had just given up our freedom to Uncle Sam and had each become a number instead of a person. Your number was your Service Serial Number and mine was 344263 and W.O. was 344264. Our new friend John Wesley Tatum (Deacon) from Coaling, Alabama, was 344273. In the Marine Corps, you had to know your SSN by heart or you felt you might be executed. The lower your number, the greater was your prestige in the Marine Corps and, for the next two years, I frequently reminded my two friends that I was the old-timer and they were the BOOTS (raw recruits).

Our new and larger group of perhaps fifty Alabama recruits boarded an ancient wooden day coach with wooden seats and kerosene lights that we felt must be on loan from the Smithsonian, and away we went from Birmingham toward Atlanta. All trains that I rode on in WWII were always pulled by steam locomotives. The diesel locomotive had not yet made its appearance, at least not where I went. We were so young and so cocky and had very little idea of what lay ahead at Parris Island, South Carolina. We spent a lot of time hanging out of the windows and waving and whistling at all girls. In fact, before December 7, 1941, we had never even heard of Parris Island. After riding all night sitting up in that ancient train car, we arrived at a nowhere place called Yemassee Junction, close to Parris Island at dawn on December 31, 1941. The only thing there was a small sign that said Yemassee Junction; I don't even remember a depot. As I recall, we had become a train of maybe five or six cars full of Marine recruits from all over the East Coast. Our train was boarded by some neat, clean, sharp Marines in green uniforms who immediately began screaming at us and calling us morons, idiots, scum, mallard heads, stupid babies, and some unprintable names that I am not sure I had ever heard before. The old world ended as we were loaded into buses and taken a few miles to Parris Island. One of the uniformed Marines boarded our bus and stood at the front facing us and shouting information and warnings all the way. We were reminded over and over again that we were "BOOTS" and probably did not have what it takes to become Marines. He let us know that Boots were the lowest form of humanity, in fact, maybe not even human, and from the looks of us, none of us could become Marines.

On arriving at Parris Island, we unloaded and marched to a mess hall with our suitcases and were fed boiled potatoes and sliced white bread and coffee for breakfast with the uniformed Marine still screaming at us the whole five minutes of eating time. We noted anyone casually walking by and not in ranks or formation would always shout "YOU'LL BE SOR-REE!" We were then lined up outside the mess hall and our names called as we were assigned to platoons. W.O., Deacon Tatum, and I were all assigned to the same platoon. I seem to recall we were told we were the last platoon of 1941, and we were numbered 277. We were told there was no holiday celebration for New Year's Day and Parris Island paid no attention to the event. Here we were assigned our drill instructor (DI) and his assistant. Our DI was named Corporal Nelson and his assistant was named Pfc. Dillenbeck.

We were then marched over to a quartermaster supply building, lined up inside, and told to totally undress. You could keep only your wallet, which was inspected, and everything else went into your suitcase and was tagged with a card that you filled out, and the suitcase was shipped to your home. You could not even retain a pocket knife. You were then given a tall heavy canvas "sea bag" that was stiff enough to stand alone and you began a long walk in front of a counter where you received new clothing of every description. You received a deluge of clothing: new white shorts and T-shirts (skivvies), a uniform blouse and pants, shirts, and socks. You placed everything carefully folded in your sea bag as folding instructions were bellowed by the DI. Everything was packed in a prescribed sequence with your overcoat carefully folded on the very bottom. One of each item was tried on and exchanged if the DI felt this was necessary. We were told we were the last platoon to receive the old high-top Marine dress shoes and the DI said he never wanted to see our shoes looking this bad again (they were brand-new). We were then marched to a barbershop and had our heads shaved. Oh, yes, we were also issued a steel bucket with toilet articles (scrub brush, soap, sewing kit, etc.) and were told we would be charged twenty-five dollars for this. With our pay of twenty-one dollars a month, this meant we would receive no pay for quite a while. They really knew how to make us feel wonderful. "YOU'LL BE SOR-REE" was already coming true.

After this, we shouldered our sea bags and marched about two miles to our home of brand-new corrugated steel Quonset huts, with wooden floors, and W.O., Deacon, and I managed to get into the same hut. As we were staggering along carrying all that gear, the DI. constantly called us weaklings and Mama's little darlings. After arriving exhausted at the huts, he offered to "whip anybody's ass right now who didn't want to be a Marine." For the entire six weeks instead of the usual peacetime duration of twelve weeks at Parris Island, the DI reminded us daily that we were not Marines, only BOOTS. We would be Marines only when we had earned emblems to wear on our uniform blouses and covers (hats).

From that moment on, much remains in my memory as a blur of constant activity with seldom a moment of time when you could do anything of your own will. Everything was done the Marine way, even to fine details, like how to repack your sea bag each time something was removed. It was evident you were expected to be an obedient robot, who asked no questions and simply obeyed all orders from your DI. Our natural human rebelliousness was being removed and replaced with unquestioned obedience to orders. The DI was never silent and we were never still, until a short time after evening chow. Weapons were issued that first day as we marched back down the two miles to the main base. They were the Model 1903 Springfield rifle and mine was no doubt a veteran of WWI and numbered 345293. This number was also committed to memory to be given on a second's notice to the DI. Our clothing for that January and February was always cotton khaki pants and shirt and sweatshirt and pith helmets with no emblem on the helmet. No one dared complain of being cold because that only brought on more vigorous exercise.

We began to learn that a large number of the boys in our platoon were from Boston, Massachusetts, and we had a great time kidding one another about accents. We were not allowed to go anywhere away from our hut area. Our packs and steel helmets were of WWI era as were our mess gear, canteens, and other equipment.

3

*"Lord, how do you expect me to make Marines
out of this bunch of morons?"*

Parris Island can only be described as some sort of con-
trived nightmare that is very necessary, especially in time of
war, to convert silly young men into serious, useful warriors
their nation so desperately needs. My experience there was
one of which I have no criticism. At times, our DI was hard, at
times mean, but never cruel or unfair. Punishment was immediate and swift, but never to the point of being sadistic. The

message was to get it right and the harassment would stop. We did not get the feeling that he enjoyed his job at all. If he gave the command "left face" and someone turned to the right, he would bring the man out in front of the platoon and tell him to shout "Left face!" and do it in a circle until told to stop and the recruit would do it for ten or fifteen minutes while our DI drilled the platoon around where we could observe the poor guy shouting "Left face!" and doing left face hundreds of times. If someone snickered, he would join the man doing left face and shout, "I am an idiot!" over and over while he did left face also. When the DI would stop the left face punishment, the men would be halfway down to their knees in the sand, and he would make them smooth the sand when they stepped up out of the hole.

We were told chewing gum was forbidden, and if the DI caught you with gum in your mouth he would make you rub it in your short hair. We were told to have all buttons buttoned; if he found someone with an unbuttoned shirt pocket, he would take his own pocket knife, cut the button off, and make the culprit go get the issued sewing kit out of his sea bag, sit down in the sand or mud, and sew the button on right then, while the whole platoon did push-ups until the sewing was finished. The DI, of course, reminded the platoon every minute that they were doing push-ups because a moron couldn't keep his buttons buttoned. He told us to never put our hands in our pockets, and if he caught someone with his hands in his pockets, he would make him fill his pockets with sand, sew up the pockets, and march with them that way all day, which made one's legs raw and painful. If someone was caught smoking when the "smoking lamp was out," he would make the offender smoke a cigarette with his bucket over his head and standing at attention, out in front of the platoon. No one ever did this without getting nauseated and vomiting. The only time I remember the DI perhaps thinking he had gone too far was the time we were being drilled in deep sand with fixed bayonets as punishment for some trivial mistake and, on one "rear march" order, a man slipped and someone got a bayonet through his pith helmet.

We had a daily mail call before the noon meal with the DI calling out the names on letters and then flipping the mail up in the air. We had to dash out of ranks and pick up our letters off the ground. The DI had already been through the mail and if a recruit received more than three letters he had to run through the "belt line" after mail call. A guy in our hut named Cruikshank had to do this several times and he wrote home, telling his family, "Please stop sending so much mail!"

All of our rifles had leather straps or slings and there was a prescribed, precise way the leather sling had to be. During close order drill, there was an exact manner to do everything, whether it was going from left shoulder arms to right shoulder arms or any of the other dozen or two orders he might give and he liked to hear the sound of leather popping as our hands slapped the slings. One day, he decided we were not slapping the leather loudly enough, so he marched us over to a stretch of blacktop pavement, made us kneel down, ground our precious rifles carefully in front of us with the bolts up, and start slapping the pavement, palms down, in his rhythm of drill cadence. He would stop periodically to examine our hands. If your hands were bleeding, you could stop slapping, pick up your rifle, and stand at rigid attention, while he went back to counting rhythm for more hand slapping. In other words, you could not stop until your hands bled. You could slap the pavement harder and bleed sooner or you could prolong the process. He never had to repeat that procedure, and all could hear our platoon doing the manual of arms from perhaps two city blocks away.

Each DI had his own slightly different peculiar chant of cadence, and our DI would almost sing "RIP LAW RIP ONE RIP LAW ONE HUP HIP HUP" then repeat the dismal thing endlessly. His "To the rear march" was RAP HO, his "Left flank march" was LOUFT FLANK HO. His LOUFT rhymed with mouth. His command for platoon was simply TOON. One of his favorite tricks was to command TOON HALT—FAW WOOD and then never say HO. When he would call FAW WOOD and everybody would be expecting him to follow with a HO, we would (in the first few days) lean a little forward, with a little shuffling of tiny steps to prevent falling and so forth. He loved to do this and would scream, "Never anticipate a command," look up into the sky, and shout "G—— D—— it, Lord, how do you expect me to make Marines out of this bunch of morons?" Then we would begin another two hours of relentless drill, pretending it was punishment for not getting it right. I know we would have close order drill for eight hours on some days. As I recall, lights were automatically turned out at 10 p.m. (2200) and we were up at 5 a.m. (0500).

Several times when he felt we were not giving him our all, he would have "sea bag drill." This always occurred around 2 a.m. (0200). The lights would come on and he would bellow, "Platoon 277, fall out on the double in khaki pants, sweat shirts, and pith helmets." Then on command of "sea bag drill," you ran back into your hut, dumped out the contents of your neatly packed sea bag on the deck, stripped the sheets and blankets from your thin mattress, rolled it up, stuffed it into your sea bag, and fell out at rigid attention with your sea bag on your shoulder. Woe to the last man out and into ranks (naturally, somebody had to be last). This last man would have to return to his hut under the direction of the assistant DI and take his mattress out of his sea bag and then put it in again, being reminded that he had better never be last again. During this, the whole platoon stood at rigid attention in the freezing cold with the DI reminding us repeatedly we were waiting on the stupid last man. When the last man was in ranks once more, we would jog around the block in cadence, awakening the entire area, and then return to our assembly point. We would then "fall out" on command, go back into our huts, make up our bunks in the precise manner so that a coin would bounce when dropped on the blanket, repack our sea bags in the precise manner, and stand at rigid attention awaiting the DI's inspection. He would strut into the hut, check everything, and tell us we could "hit the sack," but we had better "get on the ball in the morning." One night, we had "sea bag drill" twice. It was amazing to watch the platoon gradually become a smoothly operating machine.

In those days of January and February 1942, the latter part of the time at Parris Island, maybe two weeks, were spent at the "rifle range." At the rifle range we lived in unheated freezing cold tents and spent hours each day "snapping in" where you were turned into a rifleman. The Marine Corps is very proud of its rifle training, and every possible detail of how to do everything properly is gone over repeatedly with each man doing it all with his own rifle. We were told to keep the bolts of our rifles open at all times, unless on the firing line and loaded. If the DI found a man in ranks with his bolt closed, he would take the bolt out of the rifle and drop the bolt in the sand. Then the platoon would do push-ups while the offender cleaned the bolt. One of the things at the range that I recall clearly was a head (toilet) that was actually nothing but a new galvanized tin trough about sixty yards long with water flowing down through it, all supported by new lumber. Toilet seats were placed over the trough for about twenty yards, with the lower part (downhill) end being only an open urinal. The fun was to catch those on the seats unawares and send a ball of burning paper floating down the entire contraption. Such were the joys of recruit pranksters during wartime. This whole affair was entirely without covering or screening from view as were the nearby outdoor showers, which were mandatory, even though the month was January. I do not believe there was a woman anywhere on Parris Island.

One quickly lost every shred of modesty in life as there was never any thought given to privacy at any time. This began at Parris Island and continued throughout the war. The most immodest procedure was "short arm inspection" for gonorrhea, held every two weeks if venereal disease was a possibility. My wife, Mary, made me delete the description of the inspection which is really better, because sometimes imagination is more realistic than description.

4

*We felt like convicts whose prison terms had finally
expired, and we were to see the real
outside world again.*

=====

Parris Island was such a shock in my young life that a little
more must be recalled to try to tell what it was like. The Marine Corps uses Navy terms for many things and then has a
large vocabulary of its own. These terms were constantly
being drilled into our speech by the DI. A rifle is always a
rifle, never a gun. A pistol is always a pistol, never a gun. The
DI would explain that guns have a smooth bore with no rifling.

A destroyer has five-inch rifles, a cruiser has six- or eight-inch rifles, and a battleship has sixteen-inch rifles. The floor or the ground is always the deck. The wall is always the bulkhead, the ceiling is the overhead, rumors are scuttlebutt, candy is pogey bait, beer is suds, field shoes are boondockers, anywhere away from civilization is the boondocks, bathrooms are heads, all foreigners are gooks, kitchens are galleys, coffee is joe, food is chow, and this list can go on almost indefinitely. Never, never do you clown around with a weapon and never do you even accidentally point the barrel of a weapon at another person. The muzzle is always either pointed up or down and a weapon is considered loaded at all times and never empty and safe. Your rifle is considered almost sacred and you had better never let it need cleaning. Any punishment was immediate and could be severe. I saw a rifle range instructor knock a recruit down with his forearm for being careless with his weapon. You became so familiar with your own rifle that you could spot it in a group of rifles.

The Marine Corps constantly reminded you that you existed as a U.S. Naval beach assault force specialist, and that you were in every way superior to the U.S. Army. You were not the Navy's army, but were the elite Fleet Marine Landing Force. This strange pride was instilled in every recruit at Parris Island and I am sure continues to this day. I wonder if DIs still punish by making recruits scrub toilets with toothbrushes? I think the greatest tribute to the Marine Corps I ever heard was given by my father one night shortly after WWII when we were sitting on the front porch at Monterey Place in Mobile after supper, in the dark, shooting the bull. My close friend Eugene Sledge was there and asked my father what he thought of the Marine Corps in WWI. My father had been a 2nd Lieutenant in Co. K, 145th Infantry, in the U.S. Army, and had been wounded in the Argonne forest, and Eugene and I had just been discharged from the Marine Corps. My father said he had been closely associated with some Marine units in France and the Army had always noted how well disciplined the Marines were and how well they knew and handled their weapons. He said the Germans dreaded the Marines' deadly accurate rifle fire and, "We were always glad the Marines were on our side and knew our flank was safe when the Marines were on our flank."

One thing I wish to mention is the shock to a young man of suddenly finding he is responsible for washing his own clothes with a scrub brush and a bar of soap. I have been grateful ever since, like on mornings when I would put on clean clothing that my wife, Mary, prepared and neatly stacked in my wardrobe. I still enjoy every shower that I take and clean sheets every night when I slip into bed. I even still enjoy every mouthful of ice water out of a clean glass.

Our Parris Island excursion ended after six weeks with a final week of the worst weather imaginable and we departed without any pictures being taken of our platoon or any graduation ceremony. We were issued our coveted emblems on graduation morning inside, in the hall of one of the main buildings as the rain poured outside. It was wartime and nothing could be postponed due to the tight schedule of everything. Our platoon finally saw our DI relax and shake hands with every man as we filed out and into buses, each loaded with his WWI pack, sea bag, 03 rifle, and WWI Kelly steel helmet. It was back to Yemassee Junction again and some different Smithsonian wooden cars pulled by steam locomotives. We felt like convicts whose prison terms had finally expired, and we were to see the real outside world again. Whatever the future might bring, we were deliriously happy for the moment just to be leaving Parris Island. We were told we were all going to the Marine base in New River, North Carolina.

A strange feeling frequently came over me that was to return repeatedly during the war. It is very difficult to express in words. It was a feeling of safety in the power of armed might. I would get it often when marching in step in ranks as though I were a leg on an invincible centipede or some such idea. I would feel secure because of the trained warriors surrounding me. I would feel it in a large convoy or in a landing craft under full power headed for the beach. There was danger all around, but also a sensation of safety in what you were a part of. I imagine this sensation only would occur during wartime. It was, of course, associated with deep national pride with an element of "Look out, here comes Uncle Sam." It definitely all began at Parris Island where natural selfish concern for oneself was blunted. We could never return to the natural, "Me first and me only," status. You knew your companions were well trained, physically strong, and could, would, and did get mean as hell. This still interests me as an old man.

5

As I look back at my pictures, it is startling to think America was considering these young volunteers as her defenders.

════════════════

When we arrived at New River, North Carolina (later named Camp Lejeune), it was about midnight, and the train carried us inside the base where we unloaded next to a warehouse. I honestly cannot recall that we had anything to eat on that short train ride, but I could be mistaken. The month was February 1942, and the weather was cold. We were marched off to stand in ranks outside of a lighted hut that served as an office and then called in and interviewed (not by officers) one at a time inside the hut. We got the feeling that the interview was silly because everyone was simply assigned to the First Marines. No pavement existed anywhere; everything was a sea of mud. We would live in numbered huts that housed about ten men each and seemed to line up in endless rows. Inside, they were lighted by bare ceiling lightbulbs and heated by smoky oil stoves. We slept on folding canvas cots. W.O. and Deacon Tatum managed to stay with me and we were glad our trio was not separated. We found we had been assigned to H Company, Second Battalion, and First Marine Regiment. The abbreviation H-2-1 was always used to identify our company. We were told we were a company of three platoons of .30-caliber, water-cooled machine guns, one platoon of 81mm mortars, and a platoon of 37mm antitank guns and .50-caliber air-cooled machine guns.

H Company became our home, and everything we did was identified with H Company. Our squad corporal lived in our hut with us and was extremely helpful in teaching us hundreds of things. He had been in the Marine Corps about two years and had been to Cuba. He even taught us to cuss in Spanish. Our life became one of endless training and training, continuous all day from gray dawn to dark. Deacon Tatum, W.O., and I were placed in Gun Squad number 4 and we learned to quote the 81mm mortar manual almost by heart. Our number 4 squad became known as the Rebel squad because it was composed of Deacon Tatum, Murray Battles, W.O. Brown, and me from Alabama, Clyde Lucas from Tennessee, Paul Doyle from Kentucky, and Carl Ransom from Vermont. We accepted Ransom because he said he lived on the south side of the street in Vermont in the southern bedroom.

We gradually began to relax and escape from the harsh, impossible discipline of Parris Island training. The huts I have mentioned were actually a frame of pine lumber covered with a heavy waterproofed cardboard. It was possible to drive your fist through the cardboard, but the huts were superior to the tents that housed the Fifth Marines and the Seventh Marines. We had several very cold periods of weather with snows of maybe six inches, during February and March 1942.

We were in the First Marine Division that was being formed and activated on the East Coast. The Second Marine Division was being formed and activated on the West Coast. The Second Division ocasionally furnished men for Hollywood movies, so we named them the Hollywood Marines. The First Division, being stationed many miles from any large city, became known as the Raggedy-Assed Marines, a name we were quite proud of in a macho sense. At this time, our nation had almost no ready-to-fight troops available anywhere in the U.S.

A Marine division was composed of three infantry regiments and one artillery regiment, with other attached units, like amphibian tanks, antiaircraft batteries, etc. I don't know why, but the First Marine Division was composed of the First, Fifth, and Seventh Marine Regiments of infantry, and the Eleventh Marine Regiment of artillery. This designation was often confusing to civilians and the news media. When a Marine said he was in the First Marines, he meant the First Regiment. If you were in the First Regiment you were also in the First Division. A man in the Fifth Marines or Seventh Marines or Eleventh Marines was also in the First Division. Frequently, the media would refer to the First Marines, meaning the First Marine Division. A regiment was composed of three battalions, the first, second, and third. Each battalion was composed of four companies with A, B, C, D in the first battalion, E, F, G, H in the second battalion, and I, J, K, L in the third battalion. Each battalion also had a Headquarters Company consisting of clerks, cooks, messengers, communicators, etc., but they were combat troops also and fully trained. By the end of WWII, there were six full Marine Divisions but, at the beginning of 1942, there were no complete combat-ready Marine divisions.

When we first arrived at New River, there were no machine guns or mortars available for our training and we used imaginary weapons represented by pieces of lumber for about two weeks until the real ones arrived. The weapons arrived, packed in wooden crates that we opened. The weapons were covered with cosmoline (thick grease), brand-new and factory fresh. For several weeks, we would march out about five miles from our huts each morning and have gun drill and field problems all day, every day, and then march back to the huts to bathe, eat, and sleep. The noon meal was served in the boondocks where we lined up with our mess kits. Then, we would march way out on the expansive base and sleep in pup tents for weeks at a time, coming into the huts occasionally on weekends. We became hardened to the elements, and really became used to living out of packs on our backs for days at a time. There were sometimes twenty-four-hour Saturday liberty passes issued to a third of the troops in rotation and we would go to the small nearby towns or Wilmington, North Carolina, to see a movie and eat in a café. I remember one night, Deacon, W.O., and I slept on a pool table in the YMCA in Wilmington because all cots had been taken. If it had not been raining, we would have slept in a park. We even slept on marble slabs in church cemeteries. Motels did not exist in 1942 and hotels were only in large towns. It was not easy to find a place to spend the night.

The Pacific west of Hawaii was all under Japanese control except for Midway Island by now and our Seventh Regiment with part of the Eleventh Regiment (artillery), being considered more combat-ready, was shipped out through Norfolk to

Samoa in the Pacific to guard and deny the area to Japanese invasion. So, we were no longer a full division, being minus one regiment. Of course, we were not told their destination and neither were they. Next, they shipped out the Fifth Regiment with part of the Eleventh Regiment through New Orleans and sent it to Wellington, New Zealand, and, of course, their destination was not told.

About two weeks later, we, the First Regiment, and the remainder of the Eleventh Regiment were shipped out to Wellington, New Zealand, through San Francisco with no knowledge of our destination at any time. Each of these three regimental moves consisted of around five thousand men and thus was no small affair. One troop train seemed to carry a battalion; thus, the total First Marine Division movement would consist of at least sixteen troop trains. To my dying day, I shall never understand how the railroads were able to handle the tremendous job of moving troops and supplies during WWII, plus all the material for ship building, factory materials, and camp construction. There were no interstate highways and few big trucks. Nearly everything went everywhere by rail. Just before we left New River, we were given a seventy-two-hour pass to go home, a journey that will give a little insight to the wild and rapid pace of events of the time.

As I look back at my pictures, it is startling to think America was considering these young volunteers as her defenders. They had the heart, but not the experience. Of extreme importance as to what carried them through it all was they were Depression kids and had never had very much of anything as civilians, plus, in my opinion, American humor and the optimism of youth and pride in being an American. Added to this was the additional pride of being a United States Marine.

6

We had our last look at Mobile
for over two years . . .

═══════════

   As the end of May 1942, approached, we were given a seventy-two-hour pass the weekend of Memorial Day and told we could go anywhere we wanted within five hundred miles of New River, so, actually, my home in Mobile was out of bounds. The 7th Regiment left New River first and then the 5th Regiment left with no knowledge of their destination. Unofficially, we knew this meant we were going to be shipping out of the country, but they never would come out and plainly state this as fact. W.O. and I decided we would try to get to Mobile by hitchhiking and left New River by "thumb express" on a Friday afternoon. We planned to use half of our time and then start back no matter where we were. I paid twenty dollars to rent a blue uniform from an older Marine for the weekend, as W.O. and I felt this would be of great benefit in catching rides. No blue uniforms were issued during WWII unless you were on sea duty aboard ship. The uniform did prove to stop cars, and W.O. and I made steady progress south all night Friday. I recall one truck stopped to give us a ride that already had a cab full of Marines, but the driver said we were welcome to ride in the back if we wanted to. The truck was refrigerated and when he opened the back doors, the lights came on. We selected a place to sit among crates of lettuce and the driver turned off the refrigeration unit, bolted the doors from the outside, leaving us in total darkness, and away we went. W.O. smoked cigarettes, and I even lit several of his to give us a little glow of light for company. We knew if there was a wreck or if the truck turned over, we were dead. Most rides were fewer than fifty miles, and we seemed to be constantly changing vehicles.

Most people were glad to give servicemen a ride, and we would repeat our story over and over again, taking turns telling it, and trying to sleep if even for just a few minutes. We finally arrived in Mobile with just over twenty-four hours to spend before we had to begin the return trip. I did not sleep at all and spent every minute with family and friends. After twenty-four hours, Corporal Don Rouse, of H-2-1, arrived at my house from his home in Biloxi to make the return trip with us to New River. He had hitchhiked south to Biloxi by himself. Rouse had been in the Marine Corps about two years. The three of us said goodbye to my family, and my father took us through the new Bankhead Tunnel before he let us out. We had our last look at Mobile for over two years; Rouse would not return from the Pacific.

The three of us did not make as steady progress on the return trip as we had coming south, because there just wasn't much traffic heading north. I was tired of the hot wool blue uniform and wearing khaki. Two would sleep beside the road while one would hold out a thumb for the occasional traffic. In Atlanta, Rouse telegraphed ahead that we would be late in getting back, but we were on the way. We were due at 6 a.m. (0600) on Tuesday and finally got there about 2 p.m. (1400), but much of H Company had the same problem and no disciplinary action resulted. We left New River a few days later after being issued new steel helmets in place of the old WWI type.

We went into fine, beautiful Pullman railroad cars and Deacon and I shared a lower berth. We had a dining car attached in the middle of the train at mealtime. We were treated to some high-style living with porters to make our berths with clean sheets each night. Our mortar platoon of about sixty-five men was all in one car. This was the first really long train ride for most of these Depression-era kids and they truly enjoyed it. Through the mountains of Kentucky and up the steep grades, even with two steam locomotives attached, the train would sometimes slow to a walking pace, and a few clowns would jump off and pretend to help the locomotives by pushing the car. Soon, some sergeant would order them back aboard with a loud profane tongue-lashing. There was a caboose attached to the end of the train for the train crew to ride in and since our mortar platoon car was the last car in the train, the caboose was right behind our car. Deacon and I were enjoying the view from the back of the caboose when we unexpectedly entered a long tunnel in Kentucky. We found the guys had locked the door on the caboose and we could not get back inside, so Deacon and I were on the back of that caboose in a long tunnel with two steam locomotives belching black smoke. We sat down in the dark and took off our green blouses and covered our heads with them and breathed through the cloth. When we came out of the tunnel and could get back inside, Deacon and I looked as if we were made up for a minstrel show with Al Jolson, our faces were that dirty. The rest of the platoon thought it was hilarious, and, naturally, nobody knew who had locked us out. We decided that was why it was a court martial offense to have any live ammunition unless issued, because I think we would have killed the whole bunch. As the train trip continued, everyone could tell we were some kind of high priority as we almost never went into a siding and every train seemed to clear the tracks for us.

Across Texas the train really went into overdrive with two big passenger engines giving all they had. Deacon knew what a mile post was and clocked our speed at 110 miles per hour, which the train crew verified. One Marine observed Texas "was nothing but miles and miles of nothing but miles and miles of nothing." In June 1942, the train equipment we were riding and the tracks and road beds were in first-class condition. As we entered the Rocky Mountains, they hooked two giant locomotives on the front with double sets of pistons and drivers on each side and had a regular locomotive attached on the rear whose headlight almost touched the caboose. The engine on the rear would transfer its power in a strange hammering way that was almost painful as it slammed us up the mountain. We left the caboose and went forward into our car to let the caboose act as a sort of shock absorber. This train trip across my nation was, for me, one of pure delight and pride in the railroad industry. I became a steam train buff for life. It is still a wonder to me how we all survived the smoke of those days—trains, ships, cigarettes, industry, trash fires, garbage dumps, and all.

They brought us into Oakland and then transferred us to buses for a trip across the Oakland Bay Bridge to the docks of San Francisco. I recall how astonished I was to see streetcars crossing the Oakland Bay Bridge. We (our battalion, E,F,G, and H Companies) went aboard the old regular Navy transport U.S.S. *George F. Elliott* designated AP-13, an ominous number we did not particularly care for. A Navy troop ship was crowded, crowded, crowded always and everywhere, everything is painted gray, everything. Our compartment was two decks below and its entrance on the port side forward of the bridge. Bunks were wire racks five high and side by side. Forget privacy, forget odors, forget everything; sleep with your weapon, sleep with your pack, sleep with your life jacket; no sheets, just your green USMC blankets with your name stenciled on them with white paint; sleep in your clothing with your name stenciled on it with black paint; sleep with your steel helmet on your head if you cannot find any place to hang it. Everything we had was stenciled with a number inside of a diamond to discourage theft; my number, I recall, was 444. Our precious sea bags were stored away somewhere in the cargo hold. Toilet facilities for all were in one room called a "head" (latrine) with maybe twenty toilet seats side by side overflowing troughs of sea water. There were two or three steel urinals, maybe twenty feet long with no partitions. There were maybe twenty showers side by side with no partitions and no place to hang your clothes. You went to the shower naked. There was fresh water in the pipes while in port but salt water showers after leaving the dock.

7

*As we went by close to Alcatraz, some comedian
waved to a man on the dock and shouted "Hey,
Lucky, want to trade places?"*

========

We stayed in San Francisco about ten days living aboard
the *Elliott* as it was being loaded, and they allowed us to go on
liberty several times. At the time, our pay was twenty-one dollars a month, and we had just gone home before leaving New
River, so we were about as broke as can be imagined. Some-
how, I suppose my father must have given me twenty dollars

or so and while in San Francisco I visited a used-book store, bought some Civil War books, and mailed them home. I have always been a Civil War buff. I asked the bookstore to wait about three weeks before mailing them as we were instructed to mail no letters, make no phone calls, or send any telegrams, and were told if caught it was a court martial offense and that the mails were being watched—but we believed them. One thing I clearly recall was the news boys selling extras with the news about the U.S. Navy victory at Midway. We were given a G.I. postcard with a simple message printed on it saying we were going overseas and listing our new mailing address. We could sign the card, but that was all. From the day we sailed, all mail was censored.

The *Elliott* moved away from the dock and anchored in San Francisco Bay. We had not had to handle any of the cargo loading. After a day or two, our convoy was completed and we steamed by Alcatraz prison on a sunny afternoon and out into the Pacific. As we went by close to Alcatraz, some comedian waved to a man on the dock and shouted "Hey, Lucky, want to trade places?" It was windy, and the sea was rough, and all of those drunken Marines who had sneaked whiskey aboard got seasick and vomited in the head before they could get to the troughs. The drains in the deck of the head became plugged with vomitus and the foul mess would slosh across the deck in the head and splash up the bulkheads (walls) in the head, so

W.O., Deacon, and I went topside to the bow area and spent the first night sleeping on the steel deck with our precious blankets and nasty life jackets. We were not yet accustomed to the odors in the troop compartment. A life jacket had to be worn or tied around your waist at all times, and they were old, dark, blue, slick, and grimy beyond imagination.

Food was terrible and sparse. There were two meals a day. Breakfast would rotate, oatmeal in a bowl with a dipper of powdered milk and coffee, the next morning, a frankfurter that could not be cut, but had to be bitten off to get a piece in your mouth and two small boiled potatoes. The wits would announce the frankfurters were packaged in used condoms. The next morning, it would be two tablespoons of those bland pale navy beans with a spoonful of catsup thrown on top and the ever-present coffee. The next morning, it would be SOS, which was creamed chipped beef on toast, and coffee. Since WWII, everybody knows what SOS is. The second meal of the day was served in the afternoon, always before dark, and, like breakfast, required one's standing in line for hours. It would be something like a tablespoonful of corned beef and those awful pale beans and catsup, a boiled potato, and coffee. The troops were genuinely hungry all the time. There was an occasional small orange or small apple, but nothing could be done about the food problem.

There was a ship's store aboard, but it only opened for a

short time every afternoon, and the ship's crew had first place in line, so no Marines could ever get any candy or crackers unless bought from the sailors at a dollar a candy bar. There was no shortage of cigarettes and they were obtainable tax-free from outside of the ship's store at six cents a pack or fifty cents a carton. There were weird brands like Wings or Chelsea or Old Gold or Picayune that would be the only cigarettes sold that day. There would be days it seemed for each brand. Camels, Chesterfield, and Lucky Strike would occasionally have their day. There was the usual no love between the sailors and the Marines.

There was one bolt in the urinal in our head that was hot-wired so if you urinated on it you would receive a very strong short jolt of electricity that might make your hair stand up on your head. Sometimes, the sailors had it turned on and, sometimes, it was turned off, or maybe it turned itself on and off automatically, but going to the head was always an adventure. Probably it was wired to automatically turn on and off. Also, the sailors would frequently shut off the ventilation in the compartment as we approached and crossed the equator. We were told nothing about our destination for a couple of weeks as we sailed southwest, and, then, finally, we were told—New Zealand was to be our new home for ten months of training. When we crossed the equator, there was no initiation ceremony (per Navy tradition) for us, as I suppose the officers were afraid there might be a riot if those sailors had tried to initiate all those Marines.

Several days after leaving San Francisco, I was put on a paint-chipping detail of maybe fifty Marines. We were chipping off thick coats of paint in the passageways and replacing it with one thin coat of gray paint to reduce fire danger. This was mostly "make work" to keep the men busy. One morning, the Chief Bosun came by and selected me to follow him. He was tall, about six-feet-four. After we left the group, he said he was going to give me one of the best jobs available and predicted I would thank him after a few days. He said this was my one-and-only duty and it excused me from all other duties, including daily troop inspections. I found I had been made "captain of the officers' head." Seriously, this was my title. He told me the head must be kept spotless, and he would check it twice a day. The good part of the job was that I was the only enlisted man aboard who had access to fresh water for showers and washing clothes, as the officers' head was supplied with fresh water.

The head consisted of a compartment about twenty by thirty feet, one deck down beneath the bridge area, but outboard on the port side. There were six porcelain toilets, six porcelain tall urinals, and six porcelain hand basins. The six shower stalls were steel painted gray. I would strip down to my shorts and bare feet and use one basin as a bucket and one toilet as a bucket with soap powder added and rapidly swab the whole place. I would wash my own clothes in a bucket and, sometimes, those of Deacon and W.O. I could wash myself while cleaning the shower stalls with the water spraying. I would work fast and complete the job in about an hour twice a day, and had nothing else to do except loaf and read books from the ship's library. Most nights, W.O., Deacon, and I would sleep on the deck topside.

The ship and convoy were totally darkened at night with only dim red lights belowdeck to let you barely see your way around. Smoking was permitted belowdeck and some kind of card game, usually black jack, would go on nearly all night in groups by every red light. The cigarette smoke was so thick you could barely see anything at all and was the main reason for sleeping topside. As a Marine private, I quickly learned the choice rack was a top position near a ventilator where no one could step on you while climbing up or down and you could not be vomited on during rough weather.

As we entered the tropical warm water, a bright phosphorescent glow would be churned up by the ship's propeller and we could see the trail of the other ships in the convoy, even though the ships were darkened. Standing on the stern of the *Elliott*, we noted the light was bright enough to read a newspaper. The stars at night were visible in a clear way that can never be seen near cities, and we watched the familiar constellations gradually sink below the northern horizon. I have always been a sort of astronomy buff, and I must admit I was a little disappointed when I first viewed the irregular shape of the Southern Cross. I was not expecting it to be irregular.

I should mention here that throwing anything overboard was strictly forbidden, because a submarine could track a convoy's course by even cigarette butts floating on the surface and then radio ahead to another submarine. This rule was strictly enforced, and everyone was willing to comply.

We thoroughly enjoyed watching our Navy escort, the light cruiser U.S.S. *Boise*. She would fire (catapult) one of her scout planes at least twice daily and they would go far ahead to search for submarines. She seemed to be always on our starboard side about a half-mile away. It was fascinating to see the *Boise* spin in a circle to make a smooth sea for the little scout plane to land on the water.

We took great interest in watching the flying fish and seeing which fish would skim the waves the longest distance. About one hundred yards seemed to be the record flight. Some old Marine knew it was possible to wash clothes by simply dragging them behind the ship, and, at times, there would be as many as ten lines dragging from the fantail, with someone always waiting to get a chance to drag their dirty laundry when a line became available. Ten minutes was enough to get the job done. One of the old China Marines formed a circle of Marines around a bucket sitting on the main deck of the Elliott and the crowd all began to chatter about a SEA BAT, look into the bucket, howl, and say things like "Would you look at that!" or "Did you ever see anything like the size of that SEA BAT?" When a curious Marine or sailor would bend over to look in the bucket, he was hit on his behind with a broom. Naturally, the victim would go get another innocent to view the SEA BAT and the process continued for hours. Most of the officers came to view the SEA BAT, even the captain of the *Elliott*. I was lucky enough to see a sailor get swatted before I reached the bucket.

There was a loudspeaker system throughout the ship and it seemed to almost never be quiet. All announcements were preceded by a booming voice saying "NOW HEAR THIS." Frequently, there was a screeching of the bosun's pipe followed by some regular announcement like, "Sweepers, man your brooms; there will be a clean sweep down fore and aft." The sailors took great delight in this process and, using brooms and a fire hose, would try to drench any Marine who was slow in getting out of the way. This booming loud speaker went on for church call, chow call, sick call, roll call, anything, anytime, but never for anything like music or news reports. They did not exist and, therefore, scuttlebutt (a rumor) was constant and endless, until we almost believed nothing. It reminded me of the story of the boy who cried wolf, and the loudspeaker was mostly ignored.

We were making about sixteen knots an hour in the convoy, which was about three hundred miles every twenty-four hours or one thousand miles every three days. With many thousands of zigzag miles to New Zealand, the voyage seemed to last a month. Gradually, the weather became cooler, and then downright cold.

8

In my memory, those ten days in New Zealand stand out as some of the roughest duty I ever endured in the service.

As our convoy neared New Zealand, the weather really began to get cold and the sky, gray. When we were only hours away from the Wellington docks, it was announced we were going to have extensive maneuvers with the Fifth and Eleventh Marines, and there would be no liberty in New Zealand. We were to remain aboard ship to continue our journey to the area of the maneuvers. We were there at the docks in the large city of Wellington for ten days, and the cold was like the coldest winter day you have ever experienced in Mobile. A constant drizzle or sleet seemed to be always coming down with an occasional break for a few hours. The ships were tied to the docks, similar to being at the foot of Government Street in Mobile, only Wellington was a much, much larger city.

The cold was damp and penetrating, almost painful. The holds of the ships were opened (hatch covers removed) and everything aboard was unloaded onto the docks of Wellington. We were aware that this procedure would not be rational unless there was a good reason that could not be revealed, and I have since read that not even any of the officers, unless of very high rank, were told what was happening. However, everybody knew this was ominous, and there were endless rumors of what was in the making. As the process continued, the ships were being both unloaded and loaded at the same time; if one ship might be sunk, we did not want to lose all of our trucks, or all of our tanks, or all of our mortar ammunition, so things had to be divided among all of the ships in the convoy. This is known as combat loading. We had not been combat loaded when we left San Francisco because our general had been expecting a long training period in New Zealand.

To add to the confusion, the Fifth Marines had to be put back aboard empty ships that had converged on Wellington from all over the Pacific and then had to be combat loaded. The harbor and docks were bedlam. U.S. Navy destroyers and cruisers began to appear in the harbor in large numbers. No aircraft carriers or battleships were present. One sailor was killed on the Elliott when a cable broke as he was riding an empty cargo net hook back onto the ship after just carrying a full cargo net of ammunition to the dock. It didn't make any sense by logic, but it happened and demonstrated the constant danger of rushing the program. The Wellington civilian dock workers went on strike, if you can imagine such a thing, and our general simply told them and their politicians to go to hell and put sailors and Marines on all cranes and vehicles. One wonders if the workers would have gone on strike if they could have been told what the purpose of the rush activity was all about. We felt the strike was to the everlasting disgrace of the New Zealand dock workers.

In the Marine Corps of 1942, all physical labor was performed by the privates (Pvts.) and privates first class (Pfcs.). I was a Pfc. as were W.O. and Deacon and we went into a working party of about twenty men under command of our sergeant, Albritton, from Mississippi. Deacon and I managed to get into the same working party, and the torture began. With the ship wide open, it was freezing cold aboard, and everything began to operate by common sense. The sergeant (Brit) kept a certain number of men working, would give a couple of men four hours off to walk a couple of blocks across the docks and past the warehouses into downtown Wellington to eat and maybe go to a movie to get warm, and orders to be back at a certain time and report to him. Brit stayed with the workers and kept notes of us in a little book. He would give another couple of men four hours off to sleep on the floor in a corner of a warehouse under a huge thick canvas tarp as it was too cold and noisy to sleep aboard ship because our five-high racks surrounded the cargo openings down through the deck levels.

This schedule went on for ten days and nights among freezing mountains of ammunition and barbed wire and supplies of every description. Much of the food supplies were packed in cardboard boxes, and in the weather the boxes simply melted in stacks on the docks, and everything became a sea of mush and garbage. Cardboard boxes of canned food fell apart and the labels washed off the cans. Small mountains of useless, unlabeled cans were everywhere. There were no work gloves to be issued, and we had to handle thousands of rolls of barbed wire and thousands of cases of .30-caliber ball, that were packed in dark green wooden boxes with stenciled yellow letters stating each box weighed 110 pounds. There were no handles on these heavy boxes, but only slight finger tip slots on the ends, so each case had to be wrestled by one man.

This went on for twenty-four hours around the clock. We were all young, strong, patriotic, and eager to support our nation's war effort and really worked our hearts out. If anything in the Armed Forces ever needed correcting, it was the policy of the privates, alone, doing all of the manual labor. All respect for officers was damaged under this system and could never be restored. The officers and noncommissioned officers could have at least made some token contribution to the tremendous amount of work that needed to be done. After all, the supplies were going to be used by all hands.

In my memory, those ten days in New Zealand stand out as some of the roughest duty I ever endured in the service. Late one afternoon, Brit gave Deacon and me one of our turns to go into Wellington; we went to a warehouse, found our sea bags, changed out of our dungarees and into our greens, and went to a movie and then into a grocery store to simply look around. A very nice middle-aged lady named Flo asked us to come home with her for the evening meal, and we agreed if she would let us pay her grocery check, so we went home with her. Flo had an elderly, nearly senile father whom she took care of. We had a really relaxing interlude for a couple of hours. It is strange how people are sometimes so nice to you, and you wonder for the rest of your life what ever happened to them and even what their last name might have been.

There were no young men visible in New Zealand as they were all in their armed forces and overseas in England and North Africa. I believe Flo enjoyed our company as much as we enjoyed her invitation. It had been possible to walk with Flo carrying her groceries for her in her suitcase (the stores had no paper bags) to her small modest house, up some very steep streets so that when we arrived at her place, we could look down on the docks and our ships quite a few hundred feet below. I remember the weather almost cleared for a few hours that afternoon, and we could see some snow-capped mountain ranges in the distance that looked like pictures of the Alps. Since all of this was in July, these two Alabama boys were quite confused, but happy to be away from the docks for a short time.

The Lord had been looking out for me when He placed me in the company of Deacon Tatum. Deacon was about twenty-two or twenty-three years old and infinitely more wise and mature than I was at seventeen. Deacon had been studying and preparing for the ministry when we entered WWII. As he was from Alabama and in the same mortar squad, we immediately became close friends and buddies. He constantly lectured me on my naturally sinful nature and tried to direct me to the straight and narrow. I would counter by scolding him about his constant use of snuff or chewing tobacco. One of the things I will always remember about Deacon was an event that occurred in New River in the small town of Jacksonville, North Carolina. Carl Ransom (the member of our squad from Vermont) had gotten a tattoo and, not to be outdone, I had decided to get one also. The tattoo artist had stenciled my arm with an awful-looking bulldog wearing a WWI steel helmet and the caption DEATH BEFORE DISHONOR emblazoned under it. He picked up the buzzing electric needle to begin when Deacon happened to walk by and snatched me out of the chair and told me he would "Beat me long ways like a dog!" if I ever got a tattoo. I have ever been grateful to Deacon for correcting my impulsive behavior. I once asked my wife if she would have married me with a tattoo and her response had been "Probably not." The tattoo artist said, "Somebody owes me two dollars!" and Deacon paid the tab. Very few times in a person's life does one get a friend like Deacon! Though I was unable to get him to stop his tobacco use, he did get me to eventually master chewing tobacco. I can remember the many times I looked deep into his eyes during naval bombardments and air raids and saw the strong faith evident there that helped me so very much. I am bonded to him in a strange way that I cannot express in words. Deacon became a Baptist minister after the war, and has never missed a Sunday service, always taking a vacation between Sundays.

So back down the streets we went to the *Elliott* for an all-night continuation of stacking cases of grenades and clover leaves of artillery and mortar ammunition, and moving rolls of barbed wire in the freezing cold and drizzle. We found some unusual one-foot square wooden boxes in the warehouse where we slept that we broke open and found they contained dozens of small gold-plated tin boxes containing emergency chocolate bar rations of New Zealand manufacture. We filled our pockets with these as they were delicious, and we were always hungry. The boxes had embossed on them a ridiculous message that they were only to be opened on the direction of an officer. Each little tin box was about the size of two decks of cards, and

Deacon and I noted the tops were tight enough to make them watertight for keeping things like photographs or special paper items. I carried three of these in my pack throughout the entire war (and still have them in my possession).

Throughout this ten days in New Zealand, the galley of the Elliott served only baloney sandwiches (not the Navy name) and coffee. Nobody went to the galley unless he was unable to get free to go the two blocks into downtown Wellington. I cannot remember if we were given some money or not, but I have a feeling we were paid something like ten pounds each. Deacon was always making certain that I did not get anything alcoholic to drink if we were together, and I was ever trying to get out of his eyesight when on liberty. I remember you could get an excellent meal in a restaurant for less than two shillings. We thought of a shilling as a quarter, and there were twenty shillings in a pound.

When Deacon and I sat down in a restaurant and ordered a steak, we asked for a coke to drink and they had never heard of Coca Cola. We then asked for a soft drink and the only one they had was a "ginger beer." This turned out to be a very strong ginger ale served in a gray-white stone bottle with a clamp on top. We never ordered another ginger beer because they were served at room temperature and tasted like a mistake.

Dear Reader, you must go back with me to New River for a moment and let me recall one event. In late May 1942, Clyde Lucas (the member of my squad from Tennessee) and I went on a working party into Wilmington, North Carolina, with our mortar platoon lieutenant, Carl Benson, who was in charge of the working party. We had to load a small heavy crate into the vehicle at the railroad station. Lieutenant Benson (Benny) was a sergeant one morning and a second lieutenant that afternoon because they simply had to have some instant lieutenants. Benny had been in the Marine Corps for I think about six years before Pearl Harbor, had tattoos up and down both arms, knew all of the old Marines in other companies, and had been all over the world. We all both hated and loved Benny because he knew all of our evil schemes, but he also knew how to take care of us and get our fair share of anything that was supposed to be issued to us. He was a real member of the OLD BREED and extremely important in our training.

Anyway, coming back to New River from Wilmington, Benny had the driver stop the recon car at a filling station and announced we had time for one bottle of beer and he was buying. I had never tasted beer, but stepped up for mine and took a big swallow from the bottle. I maintained a poker face, but my first impression was that mine might be spoiled and asked Luke for a taste of his. As soon as I found it was supposed to taste that way, I stood with the group and agreed how great it tasted on such a hot afternoon. I finally managed to get mine down and was quite proud of myself when Benny announced we had time for just one more and that he was buying again. I took my second bottle and pretended I needed to go to the

63

head. I went out behind the gas station to the old wooden one-holer outhouse, poured three-fourths of my second bottle down the hole, came back smacking my lips, and finished my bottle along with the crowd. When we arrived in camp that small amount of beer had made me high and Deacon was furious. Luke and I had to endure his lecture for at least an hour.

Back to New Zealand . . . as we were walking down the steep streets from Flo's house, I remembered I had told my family that whenever I wanted to tell them anything in a letter my code would be some ridiculous statement and they were to look for a hidden meaning in the statement. So, while in Wellington, I sent a letter home saying I was well and doing fine and how glad I was to get their last letter telling me that Uncle Zeke was plowing that new land for watermelons. Since I do not even have an Uncle Zeke with any land, I hoped they would put together NEW ZEKE LAND, and get the message. Just to make doubly sure, I included that my extra set of car keys (I didn't even have a driver's license) they had asked about were "beneath the baseboard down under my bed," intending to convey the message BENEATH DOWN UNDER, thinking everybody knew Australia as "the land down under," with New Zealand being beneath the land down under. Their reply in later letters was that they had taken a crowbar and pulled the baseboard off the wall, but had found nothing. That ended my attempt to communicate secretly, for a long time.

Soon we moved away from the Wellington docks on a

gray afternoon with the guys throwing all of their shillings and florins to the crowds of girls waving goodbye on the docks. Right at the harbor entrance our destroyers began to go wild and throw depth charges like crazy. We never knew if they really had a sub contact or if it was all a false alarm. Our convoy was now very large and included many cruisers and destroyers. As we traveled north, a Navy tanker came alongside and pumped fuel oil into the old *Elliott*. This was an interesting sight as they first fired a small line across the *Elliott*, and then used that line to haul over a large line and then the fuel hose. The sea was very rough and the tanker and the *Elliott* were no more than thirty yards apart with the distance decreasing to ten yards with each heavy roll of the sea.

The Pacific quickly resumed its characteristic color of deep purple, almost black, as we traveled steadily north. In a few days, the weather became pleasant and balmy, and then we reentered the old hot tropical climate. I asked for my old job back again and became captain of the officer's head with the fresh water privileges once more. We were told we were going to the Fiji Islands for maneuvers with the Fifth Marines and soon dropped anchor about a mile off a pretty green island that I think was named Koro. Coconut trees and jungle were clearly visible. The whole huge convoy sat there and war games began.

Our mortar platoon position for leaving the *Elliott* was on the starboard side aft near the stern, so we had to bring our equipment up the ladders (stairs) on the port (left) side forward of the bridge, through the port passageway, and then across the cargo holds aft of the house, to go over the side on the cargo nets attached to the side of the *Elliott*. My load included a full pack weighing sixty pounds and the steel mortar bipod weighing another forty-six pounds. Some of the machine gunners carried their packs plus sixty-pound steel tripods, so I was not the most heavily laden man in H Company. We learned to make a braying noise like a mule and kidded each other about how our ears were getting longer and longer.

9

*I looked over the side at a line of flags streaming
out from the sterns of gray landing craft that
seemed to reach to eternity.*

═══════════

    The landing craft were carried like lifeboats aboard ship
and were swung out and overboard with the ship's cranes
when needed. Those from the *Elliott* all had AP-13 painted in
white on their bows. We were actually looking forward to the
maneuvers because it would give us a chance to get off the
crowded ship and stretch our legs ashore. We had never been
on a tropical island and had dreams of finding Hollywood star-

let Dorothy Lamour behind a coconut tree. As we were loading into our landing craft, lowering our mortars down on lines (a rope is never called a rope, but always a line), a roll of communication wire got away from some communicators from Headquarters company assigned to our craft and fell from the deck down into the landing craft. The sea was rough, with the waves causing the landing craft to rise and fall about twenty feet every few seconds, so in climbing down the cargo nets one had to very carefully guess when to leave the net and meet the rising landing craft just right to avoid serious injury.

W.O. was already in the landing craft and happened to be looking up and saw the roll of wire falling down. The roll of wire was about two feet in diameter and weighed at least fifty pounds. W.O. pulled Pfc. Jontiff aside and kept Jontiff from being killed, but, even so, the roll hit Jontiff and broke his arm. Jontiff had to be hauled up and aboard with a line. Benny was furious.

In a landing, the rifle companies comprise the first wave and the machine gun platoons and mortar platoon are in the second wave, designed to come ashore right after the first wave. After each of the landing craft is fully loaded, the craft moves away from the troop ship to join the others going slowly in large circles to maintain some degree of order. The circles would be about two hundred yards in diameter, with the craft going around very slowly counterclockwise waiting for all loaded craft to assemble in their proper places. Then, on signal, the circles would open and form a line abreast and head like a wave for the beach. We had done this so many times at New River that the whole procedure was an absolute bore. When the craft were going in the slow circle and the sea was rough, it was very common for some men to become seasick. Never do I recall any Marine offering any sympathy or saying anything nice to another Marine, unless he was wounded or injured. Going in that slow circle, the ever-present comedians would talk about greasy sausage or slimy gravy just to see if they could get someone sick. Another favorite was to offer a chew of tobacco to the crowd nearest you. A strong odor of diesel fuel fumes given off by the engines of the landing craft permeated the whole operation. Anyway, there was a coral reef (just like that which disrupted the later landing at Tarawa), and our first wave could not get ashore. Some precious landing craft were damaged, and the whole landing was aborted, so we returned to the ship.

Do you think that ended everything for the day? Not on your life! Since Jontiff had been injured a couple of hours earlier, Benny had the mortar platoon land on the port side aft and climb the cargo nets, cross the deck, and go through the whole procedure climbing down the nets on the starboard (right) side and lowering the equipment into the same landing craft, which would have come around the stern of the Elliott to the starboard side. We did this repeatedly for about ten times, until it became automatic. When the day ended, we were all exhausted and had not even gone ashore to see the "pretty coconut trees," much less find Dorothy Lamour. So it was back to standing in line for evening chow and cussing our lousy luck while the squawk box screamed "Now hear this!" followed by some stupid announcement. When we were at anchor there in Fiji, they dumped garbage overboard several times, and huge sharks would come to the surface, so big we could not believe it even when looking at them. They were almost as long as a landing craft and about half as wide.

Several days went by as the biggest collection of Navy that we had ever imagined began to appear. At one time, we could see three of our carriers on the horizon. We knew this was no practice; what we did not know was that we were looking at almost the entire surviving U. S. Navy in the Pacific. The next morning, we pulled anchor and started north surrounded by Navy. Finally, we were told our destination was an island held by the Japanese called "Guadalcanar." In the years since WWII, I have learned even our intelligence knew very little about the place, not even how to spell the name (really, Guadalcanal). All we were told was it was a large island and the Japs were building an airport there that was almost complete. If completed, the Japs could bomb the sea lanes between the U.S.A. and Australia and it was imperative that this not happen. In our training, we had always been told we would land on beaches and be almost immediately relieved by the Army. We ignoramuses had no idea we were the only U.S. troops anywhere near this area and were, in the opinion of the high command, the only U.S. troops that were combat-ready, which we certainly were not. No amount of mock training could ever really make men combat-ready. There is just no substitute for the real thing, when you know somebody is trying his very best to kill you.

Ammunition was broken out and issued, and the machine gun crews loaded belts with a hand-cranked loader until all their belts and boxes were full. At that early time in the war, they loaded with alternate ball, then tracer, then armor-piercing ammo. This would prove to be far too much tracer; at night, the fire would simply look like a stream of light straight to the position of the machine gun.

Our mortar ammunition carriers were issued huge green canvas poncho-like contraptions, made on the *Elliott*, that had three pockets front and back to carry six rounds of H.E. light ammunition. These were worn over their full packs, giving them staggering loads. Once again, in our ignorance, we took the rounds out of their heavy black tarpaper canisters that protected them from moisture, and revealed their brilliant yellow color and silvery fuses. Everyone was expecting a life-and-death struggle with the enemy as soon as we hit the beach. We were told D-Day was August 7, and I resigned from my captain of the officers' head job, so I could be in on all briefings and plans. We were issued some brand-new mosquito nets that were snow-white, and, believe it or not, we dyed those nets on the deck of the *Elliott* in garbage cans (G.I. cans) full of strong coffee. They were spread anywhere to dry, mostly hanging over the side tied to the chain rail and then rolled with the bottom part of our packs to be sent ashore after we landed.

About two days before we got to Guadalcanal, I happened to be sitting on a head for enlisted men that was in the forward part of the ship on the first deck down, when they test fired the five-inch bow gun directly above me. There was no warning from the squawk box; the Marine sitting next to me and I both thought the world had come to an end. The five-inch gun was mounted to the deck directly above our heads. The concussion scared us both almost to death as we thought we had been torpedoed. Weak and trembling, we were pulling up our pants when the empty five-inch, three-foot-long brass shell casing came slamming down a chute to stop between us in a wire cage. The other Marine said "Let's get the hell out of here before they do that again!" When I told my squad the story a few minutes later up on topside, they thought it hilarious. No sympathy—ever.

There was nothing special about that last evening meal aboard the *Elliott*; it was as bad as ever. They did pass out a printed sheet to each man as he entered the galley that had its origin with our Colonel Cates. I placed mine neatly folded in one of my little tin boxes in my pack. We were ordered to bed early, but I don't believe anyone slept. They changed our uniform from dungarees to khaki for the landing, a change that made everyone gripe and growl because we all preferred dungarees because of the large spacious pockets. The khaki pants had no back pockets. I found out later our Colonel had done this so officers could tell what men were in what command. The whole second battalion landed in khaki. The first and third battalions landed in dungarees.

We were up and receiving orders from nervous officers and NCOs before daylight with the old Marine cliché of "Hurry up and wait." We staggered up the ladders in line and aft to our debarkation area and sat down on the covered hatches. The Navy served us breakfast of two hardboiled eggs (no doubt from New Zealand) and a small apple, served out of an apple crate, right there on deck. We were surrounded by cruisers about two or three hundred yards away that began to let go with all turrets. Frequently, the big eight-inch rifles would make perfect smoke rings that impressed me tremendously. A gentle breeze brought the strong odor of cordite to our nostrils and, of all things, reminded me of dove hunting. The cruiser behind us from the shore and abreast of us (on our port side) was not firing and I asked a nearby sailor why not; he answered she was the *San Juan*, an anti-aircraft cruiser. Our sailor friends came by and shook our hands as if we would all be dead before the day was over; they just wanted us to know there were no hard feelings between Swabbies and Marines. I remember the big bosun came by, shook my hand vigorously, and told me to kill one of those (expletive) Japs just for him; actually, he would be dead by the next day.

The sea was almost calm and I looked for the flag on the stern of the big cruiser behind us (off the port side) behind the *San Juan* but there was none there. I asked a nearby sailor why not and he said, "Look amidships" and, just then, a gentle breeze unfolded the largest American flag I had ever seen. We went over the side and down the nets in a smooth and orderly manner because we were so well trained and the landing craft was as still as a dock.

Ransom, always a comedian, said, "When things really get bad, Uncle Sam always sends in the Marines; my God, that's us! How did I get here anyway? Mama, Mama, I want to come home!" We had been repeatedly told this would be the first real ship-to-shore landing in history, and nobody could do more than guess if such an idea would be successful. Of course, several of the wits reminded us of this repeatedly. We formed our circle of landing craft and all the comedians began to wisecrack about enjoying the last few minutes of our life. Then, the circle opened and we formed a line. The sailor brought the craft to full power as we headed for the beach. The sun was shining brightly, and a three-by-five-foot American flag was on the stern of every craft; as we raced toward the beach under full power I looked over the side at a line of flags streaming out from the sterns of gray landing craft that seemed to reach to eternity. It gave me the old lump in the throat; Ransom was beside me doing the same and said, "That salt spray will make your eyes water, won't it?" I have always been a Civil War buff and, actually, my thoughts as I looked around me were, "I wonder if the average Civil War outfit was as young as this crew?" Their clothes were new, their packs were new, their weapons were spotless, and their cartridge belts were strangely bulging with bright new brass .30-caliber cartridges because we had never had full cartridge belts before.

Everyone carefully loaded his weapon, slipping a round into the chamber and putting it on safety. A cruiser float plane flew over us very low and as slowly as it probably could go; the pilot and rear gunner waved to us as though we were going on a picnic. We were all determined to get at least one of the enemy before they wiped us out. We braced ourselves and the craft slid up on the beach. We charged out ready to do or die, and there was the first wave sitting, laughing at us, and opening coconuts.

Naturally, we were all relieved to be unopposed and followed the column through the coconut trees and into the jungle. Wherever our cruiser's eight-inch shells had hit, there was a clear entrance trench scooped out, with a central hole about the size of four oil drums and a clear, scooped-out trench of exit of what must have been the nose of the shell exiting after the shell had burst. Our objective was a hill of high ground known as Grassy Knoll that was supposed to be maybe a mile inland from the beach. A supposedly easily fordable creek turned out to be too deep to cross, so we bunched up like a herd of stupid cattle until an amphibian tank could be brought forward up the creek to bridge the stream with two long pieces of lumber, with the tank in midstream. This was actually the Tenaru River (a large creek), but our crude map listed it as the Ilu River, and it remained the misnamed Ilu as long as we were on Guadalcanal. The names of the two streams were simply reversed (I shall simply use the incorrect names as we did in 1942). As we were waiting for the amphibian tank, I noticed a papaya tree (something I had never seen before) and walked over to examine it. Needing to take a leak, I did, and then moved back to the column. Deacon said, "You are going to be remembered in history for taking a leak because someone just took our picture." My reply was, "How do you know?" He said, "I saw the flash up ahead." I then asked why would anyone use a flash on a bright sunny day; Deacon said "Why don't you ask the sergeant, here he comes now?" A slim staff sergeant carrying a large press camera walked by and I asked him about the flash. He simply said "to fill in the shadows." My squad all laughed and made remarks about how stupid I was.

As we moved inland, the jungle became a dense rain forest, and the trail was up and down over uneven ravines. The heat was oppressive and stifling; the trail seemed to be almost always uphill, so that we had to take each step very carefully so as not to fall again and again on the slick, slippery, stair-step-like trail. When it became suddenly dark, we were on the slope of Grassy Knoll, maybe halfway to our objective because Grassy Knoll was actually a small mountain. We simply stopped where we were and were told to dig a foxhole and be quiet.

We all opened our canned C-rations and knew we were in trouble concerning drinking water. This early in the war, we carried only one canteen, and some of the men were already without water. There is no way to describe those early C-rations and there were no others. They came in cans like dog food and we believed the Red Heart Dog Food Company made them. There were three flavors, meat and beans, meat and vegetable stew, and meat and vegetable hash. They were opened with a wind-off key like sardines. Also, there was a can of large round biscuits or crackers that were sort of like graham crackers. They were impossible to eat without water. The contents were printed on the side of the cans, so there were no paper labels to wash off. After a while, the three flavors all had the same disgusting taste and we didn't care which one we had to eat, since we loathed them all. I am sure they were very nutritious, but we hated them. We soon learned to eat at dusk and not have the flies compete for every spoonful. I say spoonful because we had thrown our knives and forks away as useless. We ate through two campaigns with a spoon only, because there was no food that required a knife and fork. We were always responsible for our own mess gear.

We awakened in the morning at daylight to the news that we were returning to the beach and to forget Grassy Knoll. So back we trudged toward the beach with every step bringing more perspiration and oppressive heat. Everyone was without water and the dehydration situation was now critical with Marines collapsing and no wisecracking. W.O. slipped off his pack and ammunition vest, went ahead to the Tenaru, and came back with a helmet full of water to share. This was repeated by others and we all reached the river and fell in. I have never been that thirsty before or since, and had actually been on my knees dragging that forty-six-pound mortar bipod. We became organized and hydrated and returned to a disciplined unit again and continued with full canteens and many carrying helmets full of water and acting silly as they wasted it gargling and spitting out mouthfuls on each other; we were soaked to the skin, except for our precious weapons and ammunition.

We were proceeding in dense jungle when we heard a loud cheer, followed by another, and then another, as some news passed along from platoon to platoon through the battalion. The news reached our platoon as someone shouted, "The Japs sank the *Elliott*!" (Actually, it had been hit, was on fire, and would sink later that day). My thoughts were, "Why are we cheering? That's part of our team!" Then some Marine expressed it perfectly when he said, "Well, we won't ever have to ride on that old rusty bastard again!" How strange war can be. We were in suffocating jungle and could not see the water or the ships or the *Elliott*.

10

Thoughts go through your mind on those long,
long dark nights that can never be put into words.
I believe our prayers were for strength more than
for miracles . . .

═══════════

As we returned toward the beach from the Grassy Knoll fiasco, we angled northwest toward the shore west of the Tenaru. We stopped for the night on a rise of ground looking north and we could see the ships and water. We must have been about a thousand yards south of the shore. We were told to dig foxholes and be quiet. We were awakened in the middle of the night to the flashes and loud roar of naval gunfire and had a good view of the bay. It was the Battle of Savo Island and our Navy was taking a whipping. We didn't know this, of course, and figured just the opposite. When a ship would blow up we would cheer for the U.S. Navy. We awakened at daylight in a misty, gloomy drizzle and proceeded north to the coconut grove just west of the mouth of the Tenaru. We arrived in time to see what someone said was the cruiser *Chicago* creep slowly by, just off shore, minus her bow, and to learn the full details of the Battle of Savo disaster. The cruiser really looked short and stubby. Along with the warships went the total remainder of the convoy that had brought us there, with our ships not even half-unloaded. Many small landing craft remained with us, perhaps all of them. The weather remained dark and gloomy all morning and it rained lightly now and then.

Our mortar platoon was placed in position about three hundred yards inland from the beach, about three hundred yards west of the Tenaru. Our four mortars were in line parallel to the beach with our number 4 gun and crew on the right nearest the Tenaru. This was just beyond the coconut trees planted in rows from the shore inward three hundred yards from the water. We could look south across open ground directly at the airport runway less than a mile away to our rear. We were told to dig gun pits and foxholes, which we did, and then we began a process of improving them daily with more digging for ammunition pits and covered deep pits for ourselves. It seemed we were digging all the time. Between our position and the airport, a weed predominated that would close its petals when you walked through it, leaving a clearly visible trail that would remain for hours where you had walked. This was very helpful to let us know if any undesirable strangers or snipers had been prowling around. A primary concern of our officers was the possibility of a direct Japanese beach landing from the ocean, so shore defense seemed to be the initial priority with alternate defensive holes prepared and awaiting our occupancy. The third day after our landing, the weather was clear and bright and Deacon, W.O., and I walked over to a Jap tent city camp within a half mile that had been abandoned when we had landed August 7. Prepared food in bowls was still on tables and their clothing had been dumped out on the deck by souvenir-hunting Marines. We picked up some Jap writing equipment and stationery and I cut some insignias off some of the uniforms and put them in my little tin boxes. I poked around in a pile of ashes where there had been a fire and retrieved two Jap officers' belt buckles that I kept and still have. The whole camp smelled like Colgate tooth powder, which I never understood about the Japs.

I recall some Navy corpsmen were bandaging some badly burned U.S. sailors mummy-style there on the beach without even a tent to work in. I supposed they were survivors from the Savo disaster and were evacuated someway, if they survived. Their burns were extensive. Most of the partial unloading of our supplies was still on the beach, and we began to have daily working parties moving the stuff to storage areas near the airport on Jap flatbed trucks. A road developed about a block from the water, running parallel to the beach throughout the coconut plantation; one morning, we heard a high-pitched, shrill, monotone screech of a steam whistle and down the beach road came a large Jap steam roller that some proud Marine had fired up and had running like a sewing machine. He had painted UNDER NEW MANAGEMENT on the sides of it and you could tell he was tremendously pleased with himself and enjoying his aimless ride just to show off. He was sitting in the cab, smoking a cigarette, with an expression on his face of total boredom. His audience gave him an approving cheer. The machine was a constant work horse on the airport from then on. This same Marine was always driving it and reading the Jap gauges and telling what they had to mean. The Jap trucks soon carried the same UNDER NEW MANAGE-MENT signs painted on them as did an ice plant that was painted TOJO ICE PLANT—UNDER NEW MANAGEMENT. We never did see any ice and I am not sure there was any. All of the coconut trees had been planted in rows like a checkerboard.

Air raids began daily, sometimes twice or even three times daily. Our position was just about a hundred yards beyond the southern edge of the coconut plantation and sometimes we would be strafed by Zeros, as we had no planes of our own.

When these Zeros would fly over us, everyone would fire at them from their deep foxholes with their own weapons and scream curses and threats. I don't think we ever knocked one down with rifle fire, but we wasted a lot of ammunition in those early days. I would even blaze away with my .45 automatic pistol, which was ridiculous, but it pleased me.

Almost every night, we would be bombarded by Jap navy—sometimes cruisers, sometimes destroyers; they would turn on their searchlights just off shore and light up our area so that you could have read a newspaper even in your hole. They were hoping to get us to return fire and give away our positions. This might go on for several hours. We felt like we were in a shooting gallery at a carnival and we were the stationary targets. If there were no casualties in the platoon, there would be comments like "Those Jap gunners couldn't hit a bull in the ass with a bass fiddle!" There were even submarines in broad daylight throwing shells in at us. We learned safety consisted of being beneath the surface during air raids or bombardments. If you were beneath the surface, you would survive almost anything, except a direct hit. Everyone on the island had his numerous near-miss stories. We never went anywhere without our weapons and helmets and always knew the locations of nearby holes to jump into.

On daily working parties, weapons were neatly stacked close by in threes with the stacking swivels. Your weapon became a part of you; you slept with it, a round in the chamber, on safety. When someone announced he was going to the head, he would go with his weapon and helmet. A comedian would call out, "Be sure to wear your cartridge belt in case you fall in so we will have a clue as to what to pull out!" There was never anything nice to say, no sympathy or respect.

When the first air raids began, we would stand out to observe the show and watch our 90mm anti-aircraft battery fire. The battery was close to our position and the loud noise when they fired was almost painful. Soon, a piece of 90mm shrapnel landed on our Jap wash basin and it jumped about thirty feet into the air, telling us to get under cover. We learned we could watch the show for a while, until the shrapnel had time to start reaching the ground. In those early days, the anti-aircraft battery would sometimes be way off-target and, when we walked past the battery going on a working party, some comedian would call out and ask them if the scuttlebutt was true that they had left their sights aboard ship—no sympathy, nothing nice to say, and such foul language. As we walked by, some comedian would shout, "I bet your mother doesn't know you use those bad words!" The anti-aircraft battery soon became deadly in their accurate fire and knocked down quite a few bombers that we observed. We would tell them they were getting better.

In those early days of August, we did not have enough troops to defend a complete perimeter of the airport and had to settle for beach defenses and solid defensive positions on both flanks, leaving the back of the airport where hills and ridges predominated, undefended in part. It was not wide open, but had scattered strong points, like surrounding artillery batteries. A large part of our division was still over on the island of Tulagi and, of course, the whole Seventh Regiment was still on Samoa. Tulagi and Guadalcanal were some fifteen miles apart in distance. Landing craft could be used to ferry troops across this, which became known as Iron Bottom Bay. Naval battles were out in the bay, so to speak.

We had primary positions and secondary positions we could occupy on the beach. About this time, the hated C-rations ran out and we began a battalion mess for chow. The Japs had left a warehouse full of rice in woven square grass bags, three feet square by about a foot thick. Without this rice, we might not have made it. My recollection of the pile of rice is that it would have filled about eight eighteen-wheeler trailers. We had it twice a day, about two tablespoons full each meal, and food became the main topic of every thought and conversation. The rice contained white worms or some kind of creature with short legs about the same size as the rice grains, but a little fatter, and, after a short time, nobody ever bothered to separate them. We were truly hungry and there was no food to be found. We were always involved in hard physical labor and needed calories. Many coconuts were consumed and this resulted in violent, profuse diarrhea, which may have had some pathology in some of the worse cases like salmonella. W.O. became emaciated and could not stand, so I had to nurse him like a baby, but with no kind words or sympathy, being careful to tell him what a pain he was and how we all wished he would quit goofing off and pretending to be sick just to get out of working. The hospital (a large screened Jap tent), with no cots and patients lying on the deck, was much closer to the airfield than we were. They had no medicine anyway, so nobody wanted to go there because its location made it closer to the bull's-eye of the Japanese target, which was the airfield. Our company corpsman Doc Kirby finally obtained some Japanese paregoric that probably saved W.O. and several other members of the mortar platoon.

A pattern developed of searching for and stealing anything to eat; once we found a large wooden box on the beach and brought it into the area. It turned out to be WWI hard tack; inside the box was a large brown tin box about a foot deep and three feet square with a handle that we pulled to open the sealed contents. The box was stenciled with something like "Field Ration Biscuits 1918," and we started to eat the things. They were about four inches square and a half-inch thick. They had to be broken into pieces with bayonet handles and then put in your mouth and sucked to soften; they tasted like corrugated paper. We were eating and hoarding them until one was left out in the rain by accident and swelled to about four times its dry size. After that, we were afraid of them. These biscuits were always a mystery to me until I read after the war that when the Fifth

Marines' gear was loaded in New Orleans for New Zealand, part of a warehouse of supplies that had been returned from Panama by the army for destruction got loaded by mistake. Such is the confusion of war. Some comedian said he saw a case of G.I. soap that contained a printed message about conserving soap signed "A. Lincoln, President." I cannot verify that tale, but would not doubt it."

Another pattern that developed was daily working parties for half of the mortar platoon. One day you worked—and that night you slept (supposedly) in a hole by the gun pit, ready to serve the mortar if needed. The next day you had no working party, but remained to serve the mortar if needed, and that night you became a rifleman on the perimeter defense. This division was possible because a mortar platoon had extra men for ammunition bearers on a landing. All of the men knew how to operate the mortar and four men for each mortar were all that were necessary to be available at all times. In those early days, most of our working parties were digging large pits on the open space between us and the runway for burying ammunition, bombs, gasoline, and supplies. These pits were about five yards wide, ten yards long, and six feet deep. It was bulldozer work, but there was only one bulldozer and it had more important work to do—clearing coconut trees and lengthening the runway. We dug the pits with shovels with one side on an incline so a truck could back down and into the pit, all out in the blazing tropical sun.

Deacon and I were in the same group on the nights we were perimeter riflemen and we paired off so as to be in the same foxhole together. We would take turns sleeping for two hours and staying awake for two hours, which was the prescribed order. Deacon and I were both armed with pistols and we would trade weapons with whoever was left on the mortar duty that night, because every Marine felt better with a rifle in a foxhole instead of a pistol. We also found Benny was in charge of our group on the perimeter and what an experience that was. Benny would order us to "fall in," bring us to attention as though we were on a parade ground in that forsaken place just before dark and inspect our weapons, make sure our cartridge belts were full, make sure we had two bandoleers of ammunition each, and place us in the foxholes we had prepared on previous days and nights.

Then he would announce that anyone on top of the ground was an enemy, and could and should be shot—there would be no infiltration through our lines. He would say if you need to go to the head, use your helmet, and place it on the side of your hole and empty it in the morning. Then, his final cheerful note was that he was behind us in a foxhole with a sergeant and, when the Japs hit us, not to come back there looking for your mother, because there was nobody back there but Old Benny and he had a BAR (Browning Automatic Rifle) on full automatic and you would get cut in half. Then he would remind us to be sure and fire our rifles stupidly when there was no target because that would show the Japs where we were so they could throw us a few grenades. I wasn't going to be eighteen until September 2. If there had been such a thing as a meter to carry that measured from anxiety to concern to scare to fear to terror, many times mine would have been pinned beyond terror.

I was there the night the Jap scouts kept calling out "Marine, you die!" over and over, trying to get us to give away our position. Benny would growl "Quiet" in his low guttural voice so that we could just hear him. This went on for about fifteen minutes, and then some Marine in a disguised voice called out loud and clear, "Tojo eats s——t!" A chorus of laughter assured our position was no longer a secret. Benny was furious. Several times, when we were in those foxholes, we would have rain storms and there was nothing to do except lie there, take it, and shiver with cold. Some comedian would sing in a low voice, "It isn't raining rain to me; it's raining daffodils!" This would bring a chorus of groans, curses, and suggestions that he might be a stupid, Asiatic, illegitimate, and worthless direct descendant of a female canine.

We learned to dig the holes deeper on the foot end so you could bail them out with your helmet and not have the water get inches deep in the foxhole. We loved bright nights and full moons when we could see almost as well as daytime. Deacon depended on me and I depended on him. Thoughts go through your mind on those long, long dark nights that can never be put into words. I believe our prayers were for strength more

91

than for miracles, and especially for more Americans in warships and planes and carrying rifles. We had no mosquito nets or repellent. The mosquito nets we had dyed with coffee never came ashore.

During this period of time, Clyde Lucas (the member of my squad from Tennessee) and I inadvertently became heroes in the platoon. We had been directed to dig a platoon head and had completed a masterpiece, about ten feet long, three feet wide, and five feet deep, complete with a suspended pole across it to sit on. After it was about a week old and well used with all the dysentery, Benny and the platoon sergeant were sitting on it when the pole broke and they both fell in. They had to climb out and walk to the ocean for a bath amidst the cheers of most of the battalion. They could not throw their clothes away because they had no others—no sympathy, no kind words!

Also during this period, Deacon, Lucas, and I were returning to our area from a beach working party and passed close to the old Jap tent area. Deacon suddenly stopped and gave a shout—he had found a small Jap garden of turnip greens. We pulled every stem and hurried to the camp area, cleaned them with sea water, and then cooked them in our trusty, shiny, square five-gallon gas can we used for cooking stew. We had a feast to the astonishment of the "Boston boys," who were certain we were insane.

Supplies began to reach the island in small amounts. There

was no harbor and no dock, so everything had to be unloaded from ships into landing craft and then unloaded again at the beach and then loaded again into trucks. The food sent in consisted mostly of the hated C-rations and corned beef. The corned beef was in large red gallon-sized rectangular cans and from Argentina. The other supplies were ammunition of all descriptions, barbed wire, barbed-wire steel posts, aviation gasoline, and diesel fuel. We all knew the supplies were vital and worked hard to get them ashore, whether we were aboard ship or on the beach. If aboard ship, it was understood your duty was to try to steal or trade for anything useful—food or tobacco or clothing. The work was dangerous and we were always alert to any possible problem as the landing craft was pitching wildly in rough water.

The pattern emerged that the most prestige went to the greatest thieves who always returned to the platoon area and shared their booty with the rest of the platoon. The platoon became your family. Great stories abounded, like the Marine who traded another Marine from a different company some valuable souvenirs for a gallon can of peaches and that night opened the can to find it contained sauerkraut. The labels had been carefully soaked off and switched. No one had any money, and money had no value unless it was Jap money that would buy much booty if you could get aboard ship on a working party.

On Sunday mornings, Deacon began to hold worship services on the open ground in the coconut trees. He announced attendance was an order for number 4 gun squad (Deacon was made "acting" corporal), but about half of the mortar platoon would be present. Somewhere out of his pack a tattered hymnal appeared and he would read the words of the next verse of a song and we would all sing it. Some comedian asked him how he decided what message he was going to preach and Deacon answered he could preach on any text. The comedian dreamed up a chapter and verse of scripture and Deacon opened his Bible and preached on that verse. There was always comedy.

Every night a new password was given by division order as it was believed the Japanese could not pronounce words containing the letter "L." Therefore, all passwords contained many Ls, e.g., Little Lulu, Lala Palooza, Lovely Louise, Lousy Lillian, Laughing Lamour, Lucky Lindy, etc. Company runners might have to move about at night carrying messages behind the front lines and we could hear them coming from far away as they bellowed the ridiculous password. Supposedly, one was challenged one night and told he had the wrong password, to which he replied, "Little Lulu, Lucky Lindy, Laughing Lamour, hell I don't know, just go ahead and shoot me."

About this time, one member of our platoon developed into a superb standup comedian who would entertain us for hours with nonsense. One of his favorites was to impersonate a radio news commentator; he would pick up a bayonet and hold it as though it was a microphone and give us an evening news report, complete with Super Suds and Rinso White singing commercials thrown in with canned laughter and applause. He was hilarious. He could sound exactly like H.V. Kaltenborn and would say something like "I have some good news tonight. Nothing is too good for our boys overseas, so the government has decided to send the forgotten Marines on Guadalcanal nothing." After that the news commentator would announce the regular program was being interrupted to bring us a "fireside chat" from the president of the United States. Then, in a voice that sounded exactly like F.D.R., he would begin, "My fellow Americans, I hate war, my son James hates war, my dog Fala hates war, and my wife, Eleanor, hates war. I've been in war, I've been in Eleanor, and I'll take war." We would roll around on the deck and almost cry with delight. He was very effective in keeping up morale.

11

The detonation of our shells was deafening even at three hundred yards and our troops began to cheer as we poured it on with sweeping and searching patterns.

In my memory, I have stored things as happening before and after certain events, and my memory is still recalling things that happened before the August 21, 1942, event—what we called the Battle of the Tenaru.

Before we received any planes for our defense, the Army flew in some B-17 Flying Fortresses occasionally. I remember three that came in at one time one afternoon, I suppose to re-fuel. The next morning, I was with a working party digging pits south of our position, close to the runway. It had rained during the night and the runway was muddy. This was before we had steel matting on it. When the planes were ready to take off, the lead plane roared down the runway, saw it could not get enough speed to take off, and then shut down the engines, put on the brakes, and slid wildly around on the runway. The one bulldozer that we had managed to get ashore would push down some more coconut trees to lengthen the fly path at the end of the runway, and everybody would wait another half hour to let the ground dry. Then the lead plane would try again. We lined the runway like a cheering section and rooted for their every attempt. After a couple of hours of drying and knocking down more trees (we worked between these take-off attempts), they were successful, circled the field, waved their wings, and departed.

One morning, a day or so later, we were annoyed by a Jap cruiser about a mile offshore lazily moving about and throwing eight-inch shells directly over our heads into the airfield. We watched the cruiser from a deep pit near the beach that was an alternate position for one of our 75mm halftracks. The cruiser's fire was going directly over our heads to land on the airfield behind us. As the shells passed over they made a loud sound that sort of sounded like *rickety rackety*. Suddenly a B-17 appeared overhead just a few hundred feet up (I don't know where it came from) and flew directly over us toward the cruiser. She dropped one bomb that hit the cruiser on the fantail. The cruiser was surprised and by the time she got her five-inch anti-aircraft firing, the bursts were way off and the Fortress had disappeared toward Savo Island. We went absolutely wild in the cheering section as the cruiser lost control and steamed in a rather tight circle with smoke and flames pouring out of the stern. The Jap sailors were clearly visible on the deck. After about thirty minutes, the Japs controlled the fire, corrected their steering problem, and took off up the slot to a chorus of insults, taunts, and vile language from the cheering section. We went back to our job of cutting and burning brush to get clear fields of fire everywhere and leave no place to hide for snipers. We would stack the brush and burn it with Jap gasoline from square shiny five-gallon cans. The gasoline we were told was not high octane enough to run American trucks. One morning after we were cutting and burning brush, Martin Clemens, the Australian Coast Watcher, came walking down the beach and into our lines. He was tall and skinny and accompanied by five or six of his native scouts. One of the scouts was Jacob Vouza, soon to be highly decorated. I remember we noted the .303 Enfield rifles the scouts carried were rusty and filthy and needed oil and cleaning badly.

It was in this position one afternoon when I was sitting on the deck under a high coconut tree eating a can of C-rations that the lights went out! I had been hit on the top of my helmet with a coconut frond that put a deep dent in my helmet and broke the straps in the liner. I would have been dead without the steel helmet. The lights came back on with me looking up into Deacon's face hearing my name being called. They reassured me that God was taking care of me by letting that thing hit me in the head.

We took down a fence and carefully reused the rusty barbed wire along our front. We would hang C-ration cans on the wire with a few seashells in them so they would rattle if the wire was touched. Rows of slanted sharpened stakes were placed in the deck in front of our lines that made me think of the Civil War photographs of Matthew Brady. Machine guns were dug in to muzzle level as were the 37mm antitank guns. Each day our positions became stronger as we dug and dug like moles. We were bombed at least once daily from a very high altitude and shelled by cruisers and destroyers nearly every night. Float plane Zeros would appear and strafe our area, usually in the afternoon, and everybody would get off a few rounds in reply with his own weapon. We became aware that the empty brass casings falling from the planes were also a hazard even if we were safely out of the line of fire as they would rattle along, bouncing on the ground. The scuttlebutt abounded that our Navy was too weak to handle the Jap navy—that we had been abandoned, and were considered expendable.

Late in the afternoon on August 20, 1942, we heard the roar of aircraft and ran to our holes as usual for safety. Someone screamed that they were American and I looked up to see a gray-blue Douglas Dauntless SBD dive bomber (the first I had ever seen up close) directly overhead with a large bold USMC painted under the wing. They carried the red meatball in a white star insignia on their wings. We went absolutely wild with joy as they seemed to signify Uncle Sam was going to fight for this miserable island after all and not abandon us. The red meatballs in the stars were painted over with white paint and only all white stars appeared in a few days. The sky was filled with a squadron of dive bombers and a squadron of F4F Wildcat fighters, and all those planes overhead circling created a deafening roar that delighted us beyond description. Even today I can still remember that bright sunshiny late afternoon and the thrill of the arrival of our first air cover. The memory still gives me goose pimples and sort of chokes me up. The deck seemed to tremble under the deafening vibration and noise of all those circling aircraft. The pilots and tail gunners had the canopies back and were waving at us as they banked in a circle very low overhead. Our morale soared as the whole complexion of the situation changed immediately from nearly grim despair to delirious confidence. We just knew the coach had sent in the first team—these were U.S. Marine planes.

It had been several days before the aircraft had arrived that one of our daily infantry patrols had been ambushed and the survivors returned to our perimeter and our number 4 gun squad was part of about a three-hundred-man unit that went back out to recover our dead. We must have gone about five miles out to the ambush site. We had the mortar set up and ready when an old (maybe thirty-year-old) sergeant Benny knew came walking back from the ambush site; Benny asked him what the "scoop" was. He replied our dead had all been beheaded and their genitals severed and stuffed into their mouths. It is my recollection that my battalion after that event never again took a prisoner. The hatred for the Japanese was a genuine emotion by all Marines of my battalion.

During these early days, cigarettes ran out; we were issued Jap cigarettes in cream-colored packs with Jap writing on the packs. I did not smoke, but took my ration and traded them for some awful Jap cookies we were issued along with the cigarettes. The cookies were in small cellophane packs. I remember the cookies had the letters GOLD pressed into their centers. They were about the size of a half dollar. The cigarettes had little paper funnels in each pack to place on the cigarettes to protect lips from the paper. The scuttlebutt was that the mouthpieces were necessary because the tobacco had been fertilized in Japan with human dung. The smokers said the cigarettes were really awful and one Marine in the mortar platoon even tore one open and announced they had been made from butts picked up on the streets in Tokyo. The comedy never ended. The cookies tasted like Colgate tooth powder.

Our planes arrived on August 20, and that night, Deacon

and I were scheduled to be on the mortar and not on the perimeter line on the Tenaru. We had completed an improved, magnificent, circular gun pit with multiple aiming stakes all properly marked with different target azimuths and were sleeping in foxholes close to the gun pit. After midnight, we were awakened by a roar of gunfire coming from our lines on the Tenaru River about three hundred yards to our east. Our whole Marine line lit up like a wall of fire and did not stop. We knew this was no false alarm from roaming iguanas and were in the gun pit and awaiting orders in a few seconds. The word was passed for number 3 and 4 guns to prepare to move out. We broke the mortar down, shouldered it, and went stumbling off in the dim light, cursing our inability to see very clearly. Benny was in charge and urging all hands to move faster and stay together. We moved northeast, falling into foxholes occasionally to within about thirty yards of the ocean, about 150 yards behind our front, and set up the two guns about ten yards apart on top of the deck, parallel to our front. We were in the coconut tree plantation and set up the guns to get maximum mass clearance in the tall trees.

As soon as it was light enough for us to see the bubbles in the sights, we began to fire at three hundred yards range, a very close range for an 81mm mortar; we were firing at a very high elevation to clear the trees and using no increments (additional charges used to propel the shell farther). They brought us mortar ammunition in vehicles in standard tarpaper canisters that had additional wooden crating covering three clover leafs for a unit of nine shells each. The ammo was coming in trucks and recon cars from some dump in the rear and could be thrown out right by the guns. We could not open the canisters fast enough to keep up with the fire orders and all hands were struggling with shovels and rifle butts to knock the lumber off the clover leafs and open the clover leafs and canisters. We soon had a big pile of litter near the beach and I remember how strange it looked to see all those boards with the stenciled letters on them reading UNITED STATES NAVY—GUANTANAMO BAY CUBA. Our ammunition was the fifteen-pound shell that had an optional delay fuse of one-tenth second on it that, when set, would come down through tree limbs and detonate at ground level. The detonation of our shells was deafening even at three hundred yards and our troops began to cheer as we poured it on with sweeping and searching patterns. The accumulation of unused increments off the shells is a hazard and Benny had W.O. dashing around picking them up, putting them in empty canisters, and throwing the canisters in the ocean or burying the canisters when about half full.

When we would sweep right or left, the Japs would see the mortar fire coming toward them and try to move out of the path. When they got up to run, the riflemen and machine gunners would cut them down. Our lieutenant colonel Pollack ran up to our number 4 gun and directed us to fire on an abandoned Marine amphibian tank on which the Japs had set up a machine gun on the other side of the river. We corrected range in a couple of rounds and then put one right in the tank. A loud cheer went up like a touchdown at a football stadium.

I noticed an officer walking around in leather WWI-style leggings and later found out it was our Colonel Cates. Soon, General Vandergrift appeared right behind our two guns complete with his corporal orderly who carried a 12-gauge pump shotgun at port arms and stuck to the general like glue at a distance of about three paces. I recall Ransom said, "If you want to get your ass kicked, just step between that corporal and the general." Soon some Marine tanks appeared between us and the water; a driver got out and talked to General Vandergrift, then proceeded on up the beach and across the sand spit to the Jap side of the river where they dashed around in a several hundred yard area and ground up the Japs without mercy. Our first battalion had circled behind the Japs and now moved in and exterminated the survivors. About thirty ran out and jumped into the ocean and tried to swim away with the riflemen firing until no more heads were visible. So help me there was an old Marine among the riflemen wearing a Parris Island–type of shooting jacket with sewn-on pads. I really couldn't believe I was seeing that and can't imagine how he had it there.

After it was all over, Lieutenant Colonel Pollack came over to our number 3 and 4 gun squads, commended us, and shook our hands all around. Many riflemen from our battalion came over to our guns and promised they would never again call us "stovepipe boys" and said they never realized the 81 was such an awesome weapon. The real truth was we didn't know it either because we had only fired High Explosive light ammunition on the range in New River and that was at a distance of two thousand yards, and here on Guadalcanal, prior to this, we had only fired white phosphorus at long ranges to mark targets. We counted empty canisters and found we had poured over three hundred rounds on the Japs. Our Sergeant Karp, from Brooklyn, had been killed on the line that night and Deacon had been made corporal officially; I officially moved to number one man, or gunner position. We had both been in those acting positions for several months. This meant Deacon had to clean Karp's bloody BAR and start carrying the heavy weapon as gun corporal.

I collected maybe ten range cards for the HE heavy ammunition and placed them in an empty canister for safekeeping. There was a range card packed in about every third canister. We always carried range cards in our helmet above the straps in the helmet liner and the cards would get frayed and dog-eared and need replacing.

It was getting late in the day and we were ordered to dig a circular gun pit right where we were, which we quickly did, and lined the inside with empty canisters filled with sand and standing on end.

We had not had anything to eat all day and hot sweetened coffee laced with canned cream was brought up by our cooks and served. We had left our canteen cups back at the gun positions, so we used canister covers for cups and lined up for coffee. A comedian said, "Marines would have to line up to get into Hell." A case of the hated C-rations appeared; I ate a can of meat and vegetable hash with a borrowed spoon in the dark and thanked the Red Heart Dog Food Company.

We remained where we were and slept in the pit; Lucas joined us just at sunset and began to tell us his wild stories of being on the line during the fracas. Luke told how the Japs waded across the river quietly and suddenly appeared among them. This was when Karp and Beer had been killed. Lucas said he or Crotty killed the Jap officer who had killed Karp and Beer because he and Crotty were firing at him at the same time. Luke reported he had fired all of his ammo and then managed to get a box of machine gun ammo and unbelted it as he loaded his 03 magazine with loose rounds. His hands were all crusted with blood. He said after that he had a steady supply of bandoleers brought to him. Luke reported he aimed for helmets and knocked off so many helmets he lost count. Luke was our Tennessee sharpshooter and really was deadly with his 03.

We were up at dawn and began to gather souvenirs for trading purposes. Every Jap seemed to have a personal silk flag with Jap writing all over it and a large red meatball in the center. Also, nearly every Jap had a bamboo cigarette pack cover with the letters GUAM printed on the bamboo. One pack I opened had a set of U.S. Marine emblems (enlisted) and a single Marine officer's blouse or cap emblem. I prized these very highly and have them to this day. We later learned the Jap outfit had been part of the Ichiki brigade and had been at Guam where they no doubt had rifled the Marine barracks. We found dozens of snapshots of Marines and their families and girlfriends in the Jap packs that we carefully and almost reverently collected and burned right there on the beach.

Nearly every Jap carried many condoms. We crossed the mouth of the river on the sand spit and observed the unbelievable carnage in the coconut grove. The bulldozer was brought up to the lines and huge pits were dug to bury the Jap bodies that numbered right around one thousand. By now, we had a large number (maybe two hundred) of Jap and Korean labor prisoners who were brought forward to pick up and carry the dead to the burial pits. The prisoners, looking like midgets, came marching down the beach road in formation, four abreast, in step guarded by maybe ten Marine MPs who were all over six feet tall. The MPs were all carrying Thompsons with drum magazines and calling cadence from the flanks. It sounded and looked strangely like Parris Island and we stared in unbelief. The MPs had deadpan expressions and one giant MP bellowed, "In cadence count!" which was then followed by a chorus of clear Japanese voices shouting, "Roosevelt, good man; Tojo eats s——t!" The hilarity was uncontrolled and Marines fell down on the deck, rolled, and cried with joy. The MPs had the comedy lead for the moment without any doubt, and tension was put aside once more. The confused Japanese expressions were priceless. We felt like millionaires as we had piles of weapons and equipment for trading if we could get aboard ships on working parties. We buried our dead in our cemetery, shipped off our wounded, and returned to the old area. For weeks the whole area was permeated with the stench of death as the burial pits would crack open and more sand would have to be piled on top. Thousands of birds were attracted for many days and flew around screeching and diving.

By now, we had noticed we were beginning to get draining sores on the calves of our legs and a rot on our buttocks. Routine treatment for this was to take off all clothing and be painted by Doc Kirby with a swab of Gentian Violet or Bismuth Violet wherever the need might be. At morning sick call, there would be a dozen or more naked men being practically painted violet, with me usually among them. "Hey, Doc, how about using a clean swab on me?" Answer, "This stuff kills all germs and, besides, there aren't any clean swabs." Doc was sitting on a piece of sawed-off coconut log for a stool in the open as we filed past him; he said, "Now bend over—move a little closer—not that damn close!" No modesty, no sympathy, no respect. "How about light duty for today, Doc?" Answer, "Get the hell going. You aren't sick!"

12

*As the salvos would sweep close to us, the log roof
would leap into the air with each salvo, revealing
a brilliant flash of light as bright
as noon on a desert.*

=======

The high command could not be happy with where we
were, so when a reinforcing unit of troops, probably from Tulagi, came in, we—our whole battalion—were moved around
to the southeast into a dense jungle to extend the perimeter to
the south. This was east of the runway, which was now designated the fighter strip. This area had to be fortified as part of

the airport defense and we began the whole process of cutting down trees and brush, digging pits and holes again with much unhappy "beating of gums" and vile language. We left our old area to the new troops, including things like wooden boxes we had turned into crude storage furniture in our holes. We turned to the task for our own protection and protection of the airfield.

We constructed a magnificent bomb-proof (so-called) shelter about ten feet long, five feet wide, and maybe five feet deep. It had seats on both sides where we did not dig out the dirt. We roofed it with logs that were a foot in diameter that we cut with a crosscut saw someone had stolen. We dug the logs in on a shelf so they were flush with ground level. Then we piled most of the excavated dirt on top of the logs. The entrance was from an adjoining uncovered short trench that we had dug to a deeper level than the floor of the main room so water could be bailed out with a bucket on a line and, thus, keep the main room dry. The dense jungle and the roof made the inside nearly dark, even in daylight. We felt safe from anything except a direct hit from a bomb or a cruiser getting us with an eight inch.

I don't believe we stayed in this position more than four or five weeks, but, while we were there, numerous events are clearly stamped in my memory. One thing I recall was the battalion mess tent, which was the only tent in our area that I can remember and contained a huge neatly printed sign as large as a half sheet of plywood titled MENU. Under this were thirty numbered choices for the menu, such as:

1. Corned beef without catsup.

2. Corned beef without pickles.

3. Corned beef without catsup or pickles.

4. Corned beef and cabbage without cabbage.

5. Corned beef in a blanket without the blanket.

6. Corned beef and steak without steak.

7. Corned beef and fried eggs without eggs.

8. Jap rice without raisins.

9. Jap rice without peaches.

10. Jap rice without raisins or peaches.

11. Jap rice without gravy.

12. Rice pudding without pudding.

13. Corned beef with meat and beans.(C-rations)

14. Corned beef with meat and vegetable stew. (C-rations)

15. Corned beef with meat and vegetable hash. (C-rations)

This went on and on for thirty choices of the same three ingredients. The chow line ended with Doc Kirby standing with his large bottle of Atabrine pills. We opened our mouths, Kirby tossed one in, and we swallowed it with a gulp of coffee and opened our mouths again for Kirby to look in and be sure it was not concealed under our tongues. The scuttlebutt was going around that Atabrine would make you sterile and impotent. Next to Kirby was a real Jap skull on a tall pole with a neat little sign that read: HE DIDN'T TAKE HIS ATABRINE. Comments to Kirby were things like: "Hey, Chancre Mechanic, when are you going to hold a short-arm inspection? I know you can't be happy until you do!" The galley tent was only for the stoves. We ate standing or sitting on the deck in the jungle and, of course, we ate in shifts so the perimeter lines were always manned and crews left on the mortars or other weapons.

While we were in this position, barbed wire began to come ashore in quantity and we soon put up two double aprons with C-ration cans to rattle and trip wires fastened to grenades and cans of gasoline placed so tracers could ignite them if needed to silhouette the Japs at night. We began to feel pretty secure on the ground.

Daily air raids and night bombardments by Jap cruisers continued and became almost a routine, but then, one night, two Jap battleships came in and bombarded us for hours with fourteen-inch guns. There never could be words to describe this event. We huddled in our deluxe bomb-proof shelter and repeatedly died of terror. The usual comedians were praying out loud and promising God they would reform forevermore. Grown men were sobbing and crying like babies. The concussion was so tremendous it would squeeze our breath out and make us gasp for air. As the salvos would sweep close to us, the log roof would leap into the air with each salvo, revealing a brilliant flash of light as bright as noon on a desert. After several hours, it finally stopped; we were all sitting chest-deep in dirt with no dirt on top of the logs since it had all sifted down on us. We emerged through the roof by pushing the logs up one at a time in the dark because the entrance trench was plugged with dirt. We wondered if we were the only ones still alive but, miraculously, there had been no casualties in the platoon. Whether true or not, I have read we were the only American troops to ever come under battleship bombardment. It was a long, long time of knowing you could be in the last moment of your life. With the survival of Parris Island and that battleship bombardment, I was armed for life to take all future unpleasant experiences with a philosophy of "I have seen worse." Finally, when the bombardment ceased, there was silence among the squad for what seemed like an hour. Then a comedian said, "I hope to hell Tojo doesn't get that idea again." This was a signal to me things were getting back to normal with emotion hidden behind bravado.

Another clear memory I have of this location was that our whole squad deeply carved our initials on a huge jungle tree near our gun pit.

It was probably from this position that I went on a memorable working party to the same old beach location at Kukum. While we were standing on the beach unloading artillery ammunition from landing craft, some Jap dive bombers slipped in and dropped a string of bombs that hit the destroyer *Colhoun* about a city block off shore. It erupted into a fireball right before my eyes and we could see men blown up three hundred feet in the air. I started running away from the water, thinking more bombs were on the way, and I recall clearing a rusty barbed wire fence like an Olympic champion on the high hurdles. I jumped into a large hole and looked back to see the destroyer's bow high up in the air slipping rapidly beneath the water. I then became aware I was in a hole full of 105mm clover leafs; I jumped up and ran to another hole full of supplies that were not explosives.

When that string of bombs that sank the *Colhoun* rained down, it straddled a close-by small inter-island steamship that Punchy Leygraff from our platoon was working on unloading ammunition. The little ship was perhaps one hundred feet long and Punchy said it had been loaded with ammunition to where it had only one foot of freeboard. The crew of New Zealand sailors jumped overboard and swam to the beach. Punchy said the Marines in the working party on board had tried to start the ship's engines and take it out for a joy ride, but had been unsuccessful, so they just broke into everything and came away in the confusion in a landing craft with sacks full of booty that they shared with the mortar platoon that night. They had cigars, Cadbury chocolate bars, cigarettes, and canned butter that I remember in bright red and yellow oval cans that opened with a twist key; the butter had the consistency of axle grease and was delicious.

It was also in this location that our cooks managed to trade for some cornmeal, probably from those wonderful Seabees; one afternoon we had cornbread at battalion chow. Southerners were given extra large slices with lots of "you all" Southern accent conversation. Even the Boston boys admitted it was good chow. That event was never repeated, but W.O. was working in the galley tent and appeared after chow just before dark with a helmet full of cornbread for his number 4 gun squad. That cornbread with New Zealand canned butter was like manna from heaven. We ate every last crumb and went to sleep full for once.

This might be a good place to insert something about mail call. Perhaps every two or three weeks, mail would get into Guadalcanal and nothing was as good for lifting morale as mail call. It seemed with mail so infrequent that everyone would receive an abundance of letters from home. We would arrange them in sequence by dates on the postmarks and then read them over and over. Several received notices from draft boards that had been forwarded to them, threatening them with imprisonment if they didn't report by a certain long overdue date. This would bring comments like, "I wish to hell I was in a U.S. prison with three meals and a bed!" If Kirby was present, someone would add "and some real medical atten-tion." My family was extra good about writing and I always received an abundance of letters from Mother and my sister, Katharine. Katharine was a student at Auburn and Mother would frequently write us a combined letter giving all the family news. Katharine said she always got the carbon copy, but Mother would alternate the carbon copy between us. Mother had the gift of writing and she ground out these classics at least once a week through the whole war; I learned to read them in seclusion lest I might be seen with tears flowing down my face. Another faithful correspondent was my close friend, Eugene Sledge, just out of high school. We had been two of the greatest snare drummers the Murphy High Band had ever had to endure. I warned him to join nothing, not even the Boy Scouts or Salvation Army, and he went and joined the Marine Corps, proving he was demented.

Since our position was close to the end of the runway (fighter strip), all planes taking off flew right over our heads with a nearly constant deafening roar. We could get permission to go over to the airport and browse around a great deal. My purpose was to try to find out if my uncle Charlie Tucker might have flown in as I knew he was a Navy fighter pilot on the carrier *Wasp*, and we knew the *Wasp* had been sunk. Charlie was a 1937 graduate of the University of Virginia Law School. I never had any success in finding anyone who knew him and didn't know his squadron number, which was VF-71.

One morning while Deacon and I were there, an F4F Wildcat like Charlie flew was circling the field, making an ominous grinding roar and losing altitude rapidly; it came down for a landing across the runway. The pilot sat the plane down perfectly, crossed the runway, and then nosed down when he ran into a deep foxhole, bending the prop into a pretzel. He climbed down out of the plane and, in a fit of rage, kicked and kicked the plane. I asked a nearby Marine with a ready fire extinguisher what had happened and he said the propeller was out of pitch and cutting the air like it would at high altitude, and the pilot had been unable to get the pitch to change. Incredible repairs were made by taking parts off of damaged planes. The damaged planes were collected in a graveyard and stripped as needed. Using a bayonet, I cut a small Jap flag off of a wrecked Navy or Marine plane in the graveyard for a souvenir and put it in one of my little tin boxes. I still have it today. I recall what a difficult problem this turned out to be, because most of the little flags had rivets crossing them and thus connecting them to structures beneath. I checked many wrecked planes before I finally found one that I could cut out.

There were about ten of us from the mortar platoon on a large steel barge out from Lunga Point putting brass artillery shell casings that were in wooden boxes into loading nets to be lifted aboard and into the hole of a ship. The nets would return to the barge loaded with 155mm artillery shells with round rings in their noses (no fuses) and we would stack these in piles on the barge. We were tied to the port side of the stern of the ship with a two-inch hawser up close to the ship. I remember more than anything else the ship was fairly new and not a Liberty Ship; across the stern was emblazoned in raised letters the name of the ship, and beneath that MOBILE. The name began with a T and could have been TRIONE or TRIESTE, but I am not sure. We were shouting up to members of the Merchant Marine crew, none of whom had been to Mobile, and trying to mooch anything from them in the way of food or tobacco or alcohol, with little success. The air-raid siren on the beach began to wail, and the ship immediately lifted anchor while getting under way, and took off with our attached barge following behind like a surfboard, just about six feet clear of the ship's churning propeller.

A man appeared above with an axe and chopped the hawser after ten or twelve blows to leave us afloat and adrift. We piled the ammunition and boxes so as to give us some protection from strafing and, like Laurel and Hardy, figured this was "another fine mess we had gotten into." The landing craft that had brought us out there returned and took us aboard and we felt much better in motion, instead of sitting adrift in Sealark Channel on that bull's-eye.

I must not forget to remark that I do not recall we privates on Guadalcanal ever heard the word *Cactus* as a code name related to the island. Today's term of Cactus Air Force was never mentioned back then that I recall. Aircraft were simply either ours or theirs, American or Jap. Also, I need to report that we must have witnessed hundreds of planes shot down in countless dog fights and air raids. When a fighter plane fired its machine guns, there was a trail of puffs of smoke long before we would hear the noise of the machine guns. This would look like a colon key held down on an electric type-writer: :::::::::::::::::::: trailing behind the fighter and quickly disappearing.

13

So Frank said the first sergeant made him write his folks with a sheet of precious paper and tell them he wasn't dead yet.

═══════════

Perhaps this is as good a time as any to include a marvelous story that I think is one of the best of WWII. Frank Pomroy was in a machine gun platoon of H Company and, like me, a lowly PFC. On the morning of August 7, 1942, just as we were fixing to go over the side, Frank was randomly selected by our First Sergeant McGrath to remain aboard the *Elliott* and guard a pile of H Company stuff that included the bottom halves of all the enlisted men's packs, with rolled mosquito netting (dyed brown in coffee) around each pack, officers' foot lockers, typewriters, our mortar platoon's hand-cranked phonograph with several records, one of which I recall was "Tangerine." Frank said it made a pile about the size of an automobile. This stuff was of less importance than food or ammunition, so was way down the priority list for unloading. He was told to remain with it at all times, keep it together, go with it in the unloading process, and remain with it after it was brought ashore until relieved from this duty by the first sergeant.

Frank said there was a similar situation for E, F, and G companies, so these four Marines, fully armed, got all their stuff together and waited in a designated area on the deck. When the Japanese air raid began, they went below to escape strafing and anti-aircraft shrapnel. When a Jap plane slammed into the *Elliott*, it hit right near the ship's store area on the starboard side and spun into an open hole, starting a raging fire and series of explosions. Frank said he and the three Marines came back on deck as a large explosion filled the air with paper money from the ship's store and the money showered down on them. He said he was terrified and didn't know whether to jump overboard or fight the fire, so he and the other Marines began to pick up the money and stuff it into their pockets and packs.

Soon, he said, the big bosun (who had earlier encouraged

me to "kill a [expletive] Jap" for him) came along and tied a line around himself and ordered them to lower him into the hole down to the next deck so he could survey the best way to fight the fire. They were to pull him up on a three-jerk signal. They lowered away and almost immediately a Navy officer appeared and ordered them to pull him up, which they did, and they pulled him up dead from the fumes. Frank said they joined in fighting the fire on a hose gang and after hours, even with a destroyer's help alongside pumping water, it was evident they could not control the fire and the order came to abandon ship. The destroyer was gone when the order came to abandon ship so they began to throw hatch covers overboard to float on and, hopefully, make a sort of a raft because they knew there was always shark danger. They floated around for hours; then a destroyer came by slowly and the sailors reached down from the deck and pulled them aboard. Frank said they had no weapons or equipment, but had managed to bring their packs filled with only their wads of money and their shoes. He and one Marine had stayed together, but they had become separated from the other two and still today Frank does not know if they survived.

Frank and his buddy were told to stay in an area aft of amidships on the destroyer on the starboard side in the area of the torpedo tubes; they were given water and food, and given a blanket so they could sleep on the deck. They were awakened by the eruption of the Battle of Savo with the destroyer cranking up to full speed and firing all guns, it seemed, in every direction. He said every time the destroyer changed course they had to hold on with all their strength just to prevent being thrown overboard. When daylight came, they found the only damage to the destroyer was an eight-inch hole through the stack by a shell that had not exploded. He said they picked up the dead and wounded until there was literally no deck space remaining; then, he and the other Marine were put into a firing squad with some sailors and issued a rifle for the burial ceremony; they fired all the thirty-ball ammunition the destroyer had on board. The destroyer took them to New Caledonia and put them and all the wounded ashore. On New Caledonia, they tried to find some Navy or Army headquarters to report to, but nobody wanted them. He said there was nowhere to spend their money; there was nothing to buy. Frank recalls he had about $2,200 and his buddy about $1,800. It was all in small bills and made quite a large bundle.

They could find no Marine unit at all, so they lived with a native family for a week while trying to find out what to do. Finally, they got aboard a Liberty Ship loaded with ammunition, bound in convoy for Guadalcanal, and almost purposely lost all their money gambling because they felt to have it on them could be a liability and raise more questions than anything else, maybe even a court martial as they figured they might already be considered AWOL. The convoy was turned back twice before getting to Guadalcanal, but finally arrived and anchored close to the beach to unload. No sooner had they dropped anchor than an air-raid alert began; the ship began to raise the anchor, but they got the attention of a coxswain on a landing craft, jumped overboard, and were picked up and brought ashore. They inquired and found our battalion and reported to the first sergeant, who told them, "Hell, I thought you were dead; I have you MIA." So Frank said the first sergeant made him write his folks with a sheet of precious paper and tell them he wasn't dead yet. Frank reported to his squad and they said, "Boy, Frank, are you stupid? Why did you ever come back?" No sympathy, nothing nice to say. Not even, "We're glad to see you're alive."

The final part of this story that makes it outstanding is Frank doesn't even know the name or number of the destroyer, but says if I really want to know, "I should just look up which one had an eight-inch hole in the stack."

14

Ransom lay on the deck grinning in a crumpled position and said, "Swabbies, Uncle Sam's tough Marines are a wreck!"

════════════════

Naturally, the high command could not be satisfied to leave us where we were, so we were moved to a new position in the rear of the airport (south) in the high ridges and hills. There were no trees, only the merciless sun bearing down. The terrain made fortifications very difficult and unsatisfactory compared to those in our previous positions, and we had to begin the whole process of digging and putting up barbed wire again. I recall we turned our beautiful lines we had made in the jungle over to the 164th Army Regiment, and they used them well, completely chewing up a later Jap assault in the area. We moved to our new positions one hot afternoon, progressing diagonally southwesterly; when we were in the middle of the airport, hiking in column, a Jap artillery observer spotted us and opened on us with what I believe was 150mm artillery, which scared us. We had named this artillery Pistol Pete; Pete fired about twenty rounds at us, with an interval of about two minutes between rounds. We wanted to fly, but, with all we were carrying, it seemed we were doomed; we seemed to be moving with about the speed of a turtle. Luckily, he was about one hundred yards over or one hundred short each time. Ransom kept calling out incorrect range corrections after each round, like "up five hundred Tojo or down five hundred Tojo." We could picture the little buck-toothed, slant-eyed people feverishly working their cranks and watching their bubbles, trying to put one of those big projectiles in our pockets. We were bracketed, but the Lord above must have confused their O.P. and they continued to be over or short.

There was a long winding road that we named Burma Road from the airport up into the ridges and our new positions. The good news of our new position was the steep ridges gave us natural protection from Jap naval gunfire and we had alternate valley positions we could scoot into, where the naval gunfire simply could not drop in and reach us. The whole area was covered with the high razor-sharp kunai grass that we gradually hacked down as we built our fortifications with clear fields of fire.

It was in this area we dug some cave holes into the side of a ridge and, during one bombardment, Sergeant Duffy's hole collapsed, burying him completely except for his ankles and shoes. His squad dug him out, gasping and unhurt, and he asked why they had taken so long? A comedian answered they first had to have a democratic squad vote on the matter and the majority vote was to dig him out but, he only won by one vote. Always comedy and no sympathy.

It was also in this area we finally received some badly needed replacements and where my first meeting with my life-long close friend Don (Tex) Whitfield began. Don was from Mobile and Beaumont, Texas (he had grandparents in Mobile, his mother in Beaumont), and he was assigned to our squad. Don was, by far, the biggest man in the battalion and took no sass from anyone. He was sixteen years old and had joined the Marine Corps before Pearl Harbor at the age of fifteen. He said that had presented no problem; he had simply forged the signatures on the papers.

We went on many, many working parties from this area, especially handling fifty-five-gallon drums of aviation gasoline on the beach at Kukum. Destroyers would come in with a deck load and roll the drums overboard, then race off, throwing up a huge wake to wash the drums ashore. We would go into the water and roll the drums up the beach; then two of us on each end of the drum would lift it while Tex would crawl under the drum and get his shoulder under the drum and, on a signal, all heave it into the truck where two men would stand it up and roll it into place. Food was still bad and scarce at this time and many of the boys were having malarial chills and fever regularly. All of us had many draining ulcers on our arms and legs that simply would not heal. A great delight at any time was to get permission to go wash ourselves and our clothes in the Lunga River. There were huge logs grounded in the river bed and we would bathe and scrub our clothes with a brush on the logs with big square hunks of G.I. soap from the galley, then spread the clothes on the log to dry while we soaped ourselves and swam. Then we would go ashore with our dry clothes, put them on, and leave in high spirits, talking about how much better the other men smelled.

One day, a bar of white soap sailed by in the swift current; I snatched it out of the water, held it up, and called out, "Who lost their soap?" A hand went up about fifteen yards upstream at another log and it was General Vandergrift, as naked as the rest of us. His naked orderly appeared and received the bar of Cashmere Bouquet and I let the boys smell my perfumed hand. They made some unprintable remarks. The general waved a thank-you and we kidded him about the perfumed bar, that he must have a date that night. It was almost like having God there taking a bath among us.

We were in this ridge position when Benny announced there was no more ammunition available except what we had there in our gun pits, and that a Jap convoy with an estimated eighty-thousand troops was approaching (actually it was eight thousand). Every effort was made by Benny to get our position camouflaged and we dug up hundreds of clumps of grass and spread them around on top of the ground. It was generally understood that come what may, surrender was not an option. Our stand-up comedian was a master at double-talk and, during times like these, he would assemble an audience of observers in the late afternoon and send out garbled messages on the field telephone that seemed to almost make sense, but were unintelligible gibberish. He would hang up and, in a few minutes Battalion Headquarters would call. He would answer and deny anybody here had used the phone. We would roll around in laughter, as he would point out, "There ain't no brig."

It was in this final ridge position that we observed the great nighttime naval Battle of Guadalcanal. It was like watching ships slugging it out in Mobile Bay. The big naval rifle projectiles would arch through the night like lightning bugs and, when a ship was hit and erupted in a blinding flash and fireball, nobody would say anything. When a ship blew up, the concussion would flap our clothes. The days of cheering were over because we had learned we had no way of knowing if

133

they were U.S. Navy or Jap. We knew our fate was probably being decided and that thousands of sailors were being killed on both sides.

I recall it was in this hill position that Deacon and I were returning from a working party on the beach when we passed two stacks of U.S. Army dead. Each stack was about the size of an automobile, and the dead were piled up like cross ties. Their shoes had been removed and each body had a tag attached to a big toe. Most of the dead had their eyes open and we knew they were Army by their fatigues and longer hair. They seemed to be fresh troops in new clothing. Thousands of buzzing flies were present and we quickly left the gruesome scene.

It was also in this high position that we watched the Japs run their burning troop transport ships ashore beyond the Matanikau River where our dive bombers and fighters and Navy destroyers finished them off without mercy. We actually began to feel as if we were winning at last, that we might live to get off the wretched island. I recall there was practically no wind that day and the smoke from the burning ships went straight up in columns (actually the wind was blowing directly at us and made the smoke to appear to be going straight up). When our planes would make their strafing runs on those burning transports, we would jump up and down with joy and urge them on with loud and abusive invectives.

About 150 yards north of our ridge location (toward the

airfield), a Jap "Val" dive-bomber had crashed into a ridge, and Deacon and I went over to look at the crash site one afternoon. The motor was only half buried and I poked around and removed a metal band from some metal tubing. The metal band had Jap writing on it and was a nice little souvenir. I asked Benny if I could send it to my sister and he said yes. Since he was our censor, I placed it in an envelope, not expecting it to make the trip. It arrived and she had it mounted on a silver band as a bracelet by Philip Gabriel's jewelry store. She said when she rode the train back and forth to Auburn it was always crowded and no seats would be available and she would usually sit on duffle bags in the vestibules between the cars. She would wear her bracelet and wait for any soldier, sailor, or Marine to walk by and then dangle it and ask them if they had ever seen anything like it. Then she would tell them her brother sent it to her and it was off the first Zero shot down at Guadalcanal. She became an immediate sensation and the men would see to it that she could sit down and she was the center of attention. My father said he never again worried about her making that trip when he saw her get off the train in Mobile escorted by four Marines carrying her luggage.

We were finally relieved from our hill position by some fresh Marines dressed in WWI Kelly steel helmets, carrying full packs, looking all clean and very military. We trudged down to the beach, leaving our machine guns in position, but carrying our 81mm mortars with us. We later learned we had been in the lines continuously longer than any other American troops in the nation's history. Supplies other than C-rations and corned beef were now coming ashore in quantity and we were placed in pyramid tents about one hundred yards from the beach. We dug holes right beside the tents.

Tex and I were on a working party unloading food; we got into a corner among the piles of boxes and each ate a whole gallon can of sliced pineapple. We were unable to keep it down, and became gloriously sick. We laid on the edge of a blistering hot steel barge in the noonday tropical sun and vomited and laughed until it all came up. We soon had a cavity inside of our tent filled with canned peaches, pears, fruit cocktail, and pineapple. After that, we would cautiously stuff ourselves, careful not to overdo it again.

The 7th Marines came walking down the beach from the west; as they slowly came by, I recognized an old friend, Charlie Ditmars, from Mobile and we had a fun time backslapping and greeting each other. Neither of us had known the other was even on the island, and Charlie enjoyed seeing three more Mobile faces. We loaded Charlie down with canned fruit. Charlie came home with severe malaria and elephantiasis after Guadalcanal and went to see my family on furlough. He told them everyone was starving to death on Guadalcanal, but he had run into me with enough food to last a lifetime. He never told them we had had all that food only a few days.

After probably two weeks in our position in tents on the

beach, we were ordered to stand by to leave the island. Then, one afternoon, carrying our mortars and as much fruit in awkward gallon cans as we could, we departed the hated island on December 22, 1942. Canned fruit seemed to be the premium delicacy and the most desired food for the months we had been there and we were reluctant to leave our buried treasure hoard. We went out in landing craft, just as we had come in, and I remember what a motley sight we were with our tattered clothes and worn-out shoes—a few of us had cut-off pants because the knees had worn through. Some were wearing blue Navy shirts the Seabees had given us; everyone was as skinny as starved cattle, our skin and eyes colored a deep golden from the months on atabrine, but we flashed big grins and made jokes constantly about everything. Our weapons, as ever, were clean and spotless. We came alongside of a badly listing ship, the *President Johnson*, and I recall the list was to port. We started to climb the nets to come aboard and found most of us just couldn't do it; we had to hang there halfway up, trembling and cursing. At first, the sailors were amused, but then realized the macho crowd really was unable to get aboard, so they climbed down and helped us. Some of the weakest had to be hauled aboard with lines. Ransom lay on the deck grinning in a crumpled position and said, "Swabbies, Uncle Sam's tough Marines are a wreck!"

We quickly noted the ship had insufficient bulkheads and that one torpedo would sink it, so nobody wanted to go below that night; we all slept crowded together on the deck. Tex was given galley duty the next day and cut off two of his fingers in the bread-slicing machine. He carried his two fingers up to the "Sick Bay" and asked if they could sew them back on. He said a corpsman replied, "Where in the hell do you think this is, Bellevue?" Tex walked over to a porthole, opened it, and tossed the fingers out.

On Christmas Day we unloaded in Espirito Santo, not far from a half-sunken transport ship that had hit a mine; we moved into pyramid tents for a two-week stay. We were each given a Red Cross cardboard box whose contents were moldy and useless, except for a sewing kit in each box. A crap game started and soon one man had most of the sewing kits. It was a great Christmas in that we were all glad to just be alive and able to sleep all night long undisturbed. For supper we had Spam and what we thought was rice pudding with raisins, but the raisins were only flies in the rice. We were allowed to go out to the many U.S. Navy ships in the harbor during our time there and trade Jap souvenirs for clothes and ice cream. I went aboard the U.S.S. *Enterprise*, which had a bomb hole in her flight deck and only one elevator operative. The Navy was working frantically on her and also on two cruisers without bows (I believe they were the *Minneapolis* and the *New Orleans*). I remember for sure that we went aboard the *Honolulu* and got ice cream and didn't have to pay for it.

One day, actually five or six of us went for a hike and walked five or six miles out from our tent area to see the island and, hopefully, leave the flies behind. I remember this so clearly because we found a grove of bananas, stuffed ourselves, and carried a stalk back to the camp area and tied the stalk to our central tent pole. I remember we all carried our weapons loaded with live ammunition. We did not feel comfortable without them. We even carried them out to the ships in the harbor. It just wasn't possible to get a Guadalcanal Marine to separate from his weapon or helmet.

The flies in our camp area were worse than they had been on Guadalcanal. These were the regular housefly type and, honestly, there would be five on each hand and five on one's face all day long. They competed with us for every bite of food and were in everything the cooks served on the chow line. They did not bite. It was a particular aggravation because they would constantly try to crawl into our nostrils and ear canals. We looked forward to dark when they would disappear. Some nuts would wear toilet paper in their ears and nostrils or get wisps of cotton from Doc Kirby to wear to keep the flies from crawling in their nostrils and ears.

We departed this "island paradise" on a new ship with twin screws named the General-something as I recall and went to Brisbane, Australia, where we anchored outside the harbor and sat for a couple of days, eating troop ship chow and cursing it as ever—powdered eggs, dehydrated potatoes, spam, etc. The Fifth Regiment was already there in Brisbane and the medical authorities realized they were going to infect the mosquitoes and all of Brisbane with malaria, so we left Brisbane without going ashore or even into the harbor, and sailed south to Melbourne.

Remember, we were south of the equator, so it was cooler as we went south because the seasons are reversed in the southern hemisphere. The season was already late summer. We arrived in Melbourne about two in the afternoon on a bright sunshiny day in February 1943, and came ashore at the docks. We knew immediately that we were in heaven; they even allowed us to leave our mortars on the ship to be unloaded by someone else and brought to us. They were afraid we were too weak to carry the mortars. We boarded electric trains in this large city of two million people and were taken to the Melbourne Cricket Grounds in absolute joy and ecstasy.

Women and girls lined the way as we went through small stations, all waving and blowing kisses. We left the train at the Richmond station (part of Melbourne) and walked two blocks into the Melbourne Cricket Ground (at least three times the size of Ladd Stadium, which had thirty thousand seats) where glorious, prepared fresh food awaited us in unlimited quantity. We ate out of our mess gear until we could barely move and then were assigned to a designated platoon area. The stands were roofed in places and open in other areas, so we were placed in the roofed areas where we had partial cover, except from hard driving rain.

Thousands of double-deck steel bunks had been prepared to sit in the stands with two legs longer than the other two so they were level on the staircase type of concrete construction. All stadium seats or benches had been unbolted and stored. There were no mattresses, so we were each given a giant burlap sack; out in the middle of the cricket field they had hauled in a small mountain of hay. We filled our sacks and carried them up to our bunks. Many jokes were made about the Marine Corps finally giving us real sacks as sacks. As I recall, we were soon issued a pillow. No sheets or pillow cases, but who cared as we still had a trusty green blanket with our name stenciled on it that we had carried throughout the Guadalcanal campaign. We were eventually issued another USMC blanket to replace those we had lost when the *Elliott* had gone down.

They gave us a temporary pay of something like ten or twenty pounds and we were told to be patient for a few days until we could be issued some new clothes and shoes, and receive our back pay. As soon as it was dark, everybody went out the gate on liberty, dressed in rags, with the information that there would be a roll call for all hands at 6 a.m. This process continued for at least ten days as new clothes were being issued. I remember roll call every morning in gray dawn outside the side gate by our area. There was a large sign there painted over a ticket window that read: PLEASE OBSERVE THE QUEUE.

This entered the Marine vocabulary and, thereafter, whenever anyone would try to inch into any kind of line, someone would shout: "Please observe the queue, you s——of a b——h."

Our first sergeant, Francis P. McGrath, years later told us he would call out the names of the men of H Company in that gray dawn and, although it was obvious there were maybe thirty present in ranks where there should have been at least two hundred, there was an answer for every name. He said finally he called the names of all the dead and found they were there, too. He was standing there as drunk as anyone else. There were editorials in the paper announcing we were the troops who had saved Australia and the Aussies were genuinely delighted to see us there; it was easy to be adopted into almost any family anyone might have chosen. The adults on the street would look us in the eyes and say, "Good on you, Yank! You saved Australia!" We Southerners gave up trying to tell them we were not Yanks.

We learned their accent and their sayings and adopted them into our lingo. We soon were talking to each other with conversation like: "Allow, myte, ow's me cobber to-dye? I 'ave a fair dinkum bonzer Sheela meeting me for some tucker and a pint and maybe a stroll in the park, so, ta ta, and good on you, myte."

When we were in Melbourne, an official card was issued to each of us by the U.S. government, and we were instructed to list the value of everything personal we had each lost in our packs that had been left aboard the *Elliott* that Pomroy was to have escorted ashore. The idea was that we might be reimbursed by Uncle Sam. Nothing was ever heard of this and, some months later, our lieutenant, Benny Benson, explained it as the government had checked and found the Rolex Watch Co. had never made that many watches in all its manufacturing history.

Words could never describe our wild jubilation in the beautiful city of Melbourne. The Aussies could not believe any human beings could eat so much. Steak (styke) and eggs (eyeggs) were the menu favorites and we would order a large steak with two fried eggs on top and potatoes, then eat it and order another. Their beer was very high in alcoholic content and we tried to drink it all, but they never came close to running out.

We were paid all of our back pay after about ten days and what an event that was! We had not been fully paid since leaving New River. We privates received about one hundred pounds each and we quickly mastered knowledge of their money. We simply thought of a shilling as a quarter, twenty shillings as a pound, or five bucks. Two sixpence pieces made a shilling and two shillings made a florin or a fifty-cent piece, in our thinking. A pint of beer was sixpence, a train ride to any part of Melbourne was sixpence, steak and eggs was one and six or, at most, two shillings, better known as two bob. The nickname for a pound was a quid. A guinea was twenty-one shillings, which made no sense at all. The movies were one and six; a special seat in the dress circle was a florin, where, of course, we all sat with our girls. We were millionaires. American cigarettes bought in our ship's store in the Cricket Ground were three pence a pack or two shillings a carton and were gold to the Aussies and could be traded for anything one could imagine. We could buy two cartons a day and leave through the gate with two cartons only. Non-smokers would carry out two cartons for trading purposes, even though they didn't smoke. A pack of cigarettes would buy a round of beer for a crowd at a pub.

We had showers installed below the stands at the Cricket Ground and it was on that first payday that Tex was down taking a shower when somebody stole one hundred quid out of his clothes. He went berserk and ran naked around the Cricket Ground because he thought he knew the face of whoever must have taken it. He came to me after he had put on his clothes and borrowed five pounds to join a big crap game. He came back in about thirty minutes with at least ten times what he had lost. Tex said he made seven straight passes. He insisted on giving me fifteen pounds and then went into Melbourne and spent every shilling buying drinks for whole bars full of people. I sent most of my money home with a money order and instructions to put it in the bank for me. Instead, my father bought war bonds in my name and a picture of me appeared on the front page of the Mobile paper with a story about a

Mobile Marine who sent his entire pay from fighting for five months on Guadalcanal home to buy war bonds. They sent me the front page of the paper and I shredded it quickly before anybody could see the article; not even W.O. got to see that.

When the movies ended in Melbourne there was a film and music that played their British national anthem of "God Save The King." Everyone would stand in the theater and sing the words. The tune is the same as our "America" and we Marines would all rise and sing "America" as loud as we could, "My country tis of thee," etc.

I clearly recall that day in 1943 in the Cricket Ground when they had an awards ceremony and presented the Medal of Honor to General Vandergrift, Colonel Edson, John Basilone, and Mitchell Paige. We—the whole First Regiment— were required to attend and were anxious for it to end and the band shut up because as soon as it ended we were free to go out the gate on liberty. As this auspicious event occurred Ransom stood at rigid attention mumbling, "Hurry it up" again and again.

15

From the lead car, Mrs. Eleanor Roosevelt
emerged . . . nobody could mistake Eleanor; the
thought flashed through my mind of our platoon
comedian and his "My wife, Eleanor, hates war."

==========

So much remains in my memory bank about Melbourne
that at least another chapter will be necessary. If a Marine
didn't have malaria in Melbourne, it seemed he had jaun-
dice (hepatitis A). One day at the Cricket Ground, I became
severely nauseated and weak and went to sick call. The Navy
doctor took one look at me and sent me to the hospital in a

truck with several other men from the battalion. The hospital was a magnificent new redbrick building, completed just before WWII, perhaps ten stories tall, and operated by U.S. Army medical personnel. The hospital carried the name of Fourth General. The First Marine Division almost immediately filled it to capacity.

I went into the hepatitis ward, which occupied one complete floor; there must have been nearly one hundred of us in the ward. Our treatment was primarily bed rest and fresh fruit diet. After forty-eight hours I was much better and enjoying the interlude. After a week, I was vastly improved and the no-nonsense Army nurse gave me the job of keeping our ward head clean. She was astonished when she saw how efficient I was at this and I recall she said I would make some girl a good wife. She was very strict, even hard-boiled, and, as I said, of the no-nonsense mentality, so we called her Sarge or Lieutenant Sarge. One comedian asked her if she did push-ups for relaxation and entertainment in her spare time.

I returned to the Cricket Ground where I was greeted with moans and groans from the mortar platoon and the information that they were disappointed that I hadn't died. As usual, there was never anything nice to be heard and never any sympathy. As our health gradually improved and we became stronger, Benny took us on daily hikes without packs in the vicinity of the Cricket Ground. I remember we would march around and around in the large Fitzroy Gardens that were an immaculately maintained horticulture showplace. We would pass Captain Cook's stone cottage repeatedly until we felt we knew the long-deceased captain personally and expected him to come out and invite us in for a cup of tea or grog. After maybe a month, we received large numbers of replacements, maybe twenty in the mortar platoon. They proved to be great guys.

New weapons were issued so I gave up my old trusty .45 automatic pistol for a M1 carbine. I really hated to turn in that pistol and walk away with that brand-new cosmolined carbine. Officers turned in their pistols for a carbine also and then, in a few days, we went to the rifle range to test fire our new weapons. We went in brand-new ten-wheeler American trucks with the canvas off the back where we sat, with the drivers changing gears and double clutching whenever they could to impress the Aussies. The Aussie civilians would come out of houses and stores to wave at us. The rifle range must have been about fifteen or twenty miles out of the city. All of H Company went as a unit and we spent most of the day in the process. Every man was given twenty rounds and we had to fire ten rounds at two hundred yards, correcting sights for the single shots during the ten rounds, and then firing the second ten rounds in rapid fire. The carbine had a fifteen-round capacity clip, so we had two clips of ten rounds each. W.O. and I were pulling and marking targets in the butts when the information came over the phone that Benny was going to be firing on our target.

W.O. and I, without saying a word to each other, marked and patched Benny's fire low until we had him correcting completely off and over the target. Benny was an expert rifleman. For the last five of his first ten rounds, he was completely off and over the target, but when we heard the pop of his round go over, we would pull the target down and mark him with a bull's-eye. Then, when he fired his ten rounds rapid fire, he had ten misses and we reported it with a waving of "Maggie's drawers." Benny stopped everything and came down to the butts to inspect his target. He went into a rage and cursed that lousy new weapon until the air nearly turned blue. I didn't tell him the truth until fifty years later at a reunion and he said if he had known he would probably have killed both of us.

One of the very bright spots in Melbourne was the two weeks of division guard duty that maybe fifteen of us from the mortar platoon were assigned. We were quartered in a one-story stucco building on the grounds in the rear of the Fourth General Hospital with which I was familiar. We lived in one large central room in wide double-decked wooden bunks with mattresses and clean sheets and ate in this same room on tables with tablecloths and china. The food was excellent and prepared and served by middle-aged Australian ladies. We called them all "Mother" and they loved it. I remember there were large crockery pitchers of whole milk on the tables.

There were three guard posts, one on the main entrance, one on a delivery gate, and a prisoner guard post on the top

High school senior photo,
spring 1941

At Parris Island, January 8, 1942

After the Pacific, while studying at
Chapel Hill, spring 1945

Above: Our number four gun squad, May 1942. L-R: Tatum, me, Lucas, Ransom, Doyle. As I look back at these pictures, it is startling to think America was considering these young volunteers as her defenders. We had the heart, but not the experience.

Right: Deacon Tatum and me in May 1942.

Posing with a BAR during a Sunday in May 1942.

Cpl. Don Rouse and me in May 1942.

H-2-1 member Dave Madison in the boondocks, May 1942.

W.O. Brown and me eating chicken in May 1942.

My uncle, Charlie Tucker (in cockpit), after he soloed at Opa-locka, Florida, during his training to become a naval aviator in November 1940.

Before shipping out, I enjoyed a last visit with my family and friends in Mobile, during Memorial Day weekend, May 1942. **Above left:** with my great friend, Eugene Sledge. **Above right:** with my sister, Katharine. **Below:** with my parents, Katharine, and younger brother, John, at our home at Monterey Place.

CEC/flm

COMBAT GROUP "B"
USS BARNETT

July 30, 1942.

Now it can be told:

You are now proceeding towards a true test of our combat efficiency. "D" Day and Zero Hour are near. We will have the honor of participating in the first major offense of Marine Corps units in this war. There will be a preponderance of forces and we will be strongly supported by Naval and Army units.

It is an honor to have been chosen for this particular effort and the traditions of our Corps will, without doubt, be upheld. That each officer and man do his full share is a natural duty. Only by the highest type of bulldog aggressiveness can we fulfill the confidence and responsibility that has been entrusted to us.

This war cannot be won by inertia and inactivity; only by aggressive and vigorous action can we attain our objective, i.e., the complete collapse of the Japanese military forces. That is our goal and in the near future we will signal "final objective reached".

This is not an ordinary war. It is one that demands every-ones' individual effort, as well as teamwork of all branches and units of our military forces. A person that fails to give that individual effort not only jeopordizes the success of the whole operation but his own life as well.

The unwarranted treacherous action of the Japanese on Dec. 7, 1941, will go down in the annals of history as the most glaring example of deceit and trickery of all times. Remember that we didn't start this war, but we are going to end it to our own liking. The Japanese will always regret the day they ever heard of Wake Island or Pearl Harbor.

We are fighting for a just cause; there is no doubt about that. It is for the right of liberty and freedom, and for our mothers, fathers, sisters, brothers, wives, childern and sweet-hearts, as well as ourselves. We have enjoyed the many advantages given to us under our form of Government, and, with the help of God, we will guarantee that same liberty and freedom for our loved ones and to the people of America for generations to come.

/s/ C. B. CATES
C. B. CATES,
Colonel, Commanding

Letter from Col. Cates that was handed out at our evening meal on August 6, 1942, on the eve of our landing on Guadalcanal.

This photo was taken looking toward the beach, and one can see how the green troops are bunched up, clean-shaven, in khaki, and relaxed. I am off to the right of the column with my back to the camera, taking a leak.

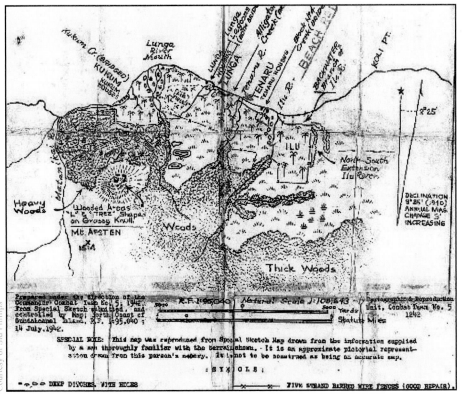

An original, crude map given to me by Harold Couch of H-2-1 at our 1991 reunion.

Lucas–
Me

There was no harbor and no dock in the early days at Guadalcanal, so everything had to be unloaded from ships into landing craft and then unloaded again at the beach.

The aftermath of the Tenaru battle, August 22, 1942.

Lt. Stratton (L) and Lt. "Benny" Benson (R) on Guadalcanal, November 1942.

In November 1942, on Guadalcanal, a member of our platoon received a package from home containing a camera and several rolls of film. Though cameras were forbidden, he took pictures and we forgot the whole affair. I did not see the pictures until 25 years after the war when he brought them to a reunion. **Above**: our number 4 gun squad, L-R: Tatum, Lucas, Doyle, me, and Ransom. **Below:** This picture shows part of our mortar platoon. I am the idiot in the second row wearing the Jap hat between Lucas and Ransom.

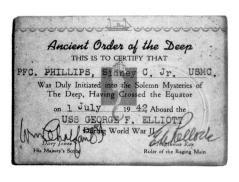

Some souvenirs from the Pacific. **Clockwise:** victory marking cut from a wrecked Navy or Marine plane, Jap soldiers' flag taken after the Tenaru battle, Jap uniform insignia found in an abandoned camp, a manufacturer's plate from a crashed Jap dive bomber that I sent home as a bracelet for my sister, Katharine, and my Ancient Order of the Deep card given to me for having crossed the equator.

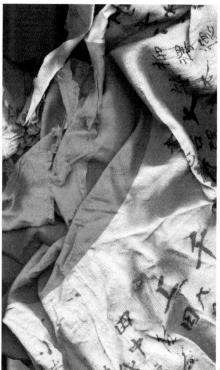

Memories from Melbourne, Australia, 1943. **Clockwise:** Cuddling a koala at the Melbourne Zoo, our First Marine Division patch designed and manufactured while in Melbourne, a photo taken by a street photographer who snapped W.O. and me eating fish and chips, and a close-up of yours truly.

On Cape Gloucester in March 1944, W.O. met a Navy photographer looking for Marines from the same hometown. W.O. came to get me so we could have our picture taken by the photographer who said he would send it to our hometown newspaper. In the picture you can see our nasty clothes hanging on the tent ropes behind us.

USMC Photo

On Dec. 29, 1943, on Cape Gloucester, we visited our small cemetery on the side of Mt. Tuali, where a Marine combat photographer caught me in a group picture that appeared in the *VFW* magazine a few years ago. It is possible to see the range cards I always carried in the top of my helmet liner above the straps.

Courtesy of Sid Phillips

Courtesy of Sid Phillips

Left and Above: H-2-1 machine gunners and mortar squad at Pavuvu in November 1944 after I had returned home.

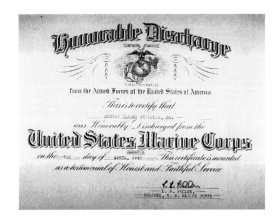

Left: My dad gives me a hug soon after my return from the Pacific, August 1944. **Above:** My USMC discharge signed by Col. Louis B. "Chesty" Puller.

Above: Mary (L) and Katharine (R) bury my friend Bunk Sims.

Left: Mary at Gulf Shores, Alabama, 1945.

Above: April 15, 1946, the final spoils of war. Mary and I were married on her 21st birthday.

Right: The wedding party, (L-R) Bill Houston (Mary's brother), Eugene Sledge (best man), me, Mary, Katharine (my sister), Betty Houston (Mary's niece), and John Houston (Mary's brother).

My family and descendants as photographed in October 2009. My sister, Katharine, and I are in the center.

floor of the hospital. We would stand these posts in rotation for a day on and a day off schedule, with liberty all day on our day off. It was absolute heaven to a Marine private.

One morning, I was standing the main entrance post (just outside the door) with an 03 rifle at parade rest, snapping to attention and coming to present arms whenever an officer went in or out. All nurses were officers, so there were no long periods of inactivity. At eighteen years of age, I was able to do this for four hours without even being conscious of what I was doing, sort of robot fashion. Suddenly, about six American khaki-colored staff cars pulled up to the curb and out climbed many Army generals and Navy admirals in full dress uniform. From the lead car, Mrs. Eleanor Roosevelt emerged, dressed in an Army WAC uniform or maybe a Red Cross uniform. I snapped to attention and came to present arms, popping the leather as loud as I could and really making that old 03 rattle. Dillenbeck, my Parris Island DI, would have been as proud as a peacock. Nobody could mistake Eleanor; the thought flashed through my mind of our platoon comedian and his "My wife, Eleanor, hates war." She walked straight to me and stopped, our eyes were level, I am five ten, and she was not wearing high heels. She asked, "Young man, are you a Marine?" My reply was "Yes, ma'am." "Were you on Guadalcanal?" "Yes, ma'am." "Are you being well fed?" "Yes, ma'am." "Are you being well cared for?" "Yes, ma'am." "What state are you from?" My reply in a proud tone was "Alabama!" She smiled and said, "I should have known," and walked on into the entrance with generals holding the doors open. I remained stone-faced and at present arms until all the brass had paraded by. I noisily came back to order arms and parade rest. Then I noticed I was actually slightly quivering. My relief came before she exited.

Up on the top floor of the Fourth General was a restricted area for military prisoners and in a large room there were four Marines with malaria confined to single beds with shackles on their wrists and ankles and shackled to their beds. We were given three rounds of live ammunition in the magazine of an 03 rifle; we put one in the chamber, and locked the safety. We had fixed bayonets on the rifles and were told to kill the prisoners if they attempted to escape; if they did escape, we would take their places and serve their sentences. I have heard bleeding hearts say such orders were never given, but, by golly, I heard sergeants give the order and we would have carried them out. Robot privates are dangerous. The prisoners were unshackled from the bed by the sergeant and only by the sergeant and always only one at a time. We privates escorted them to the head where shackles were worn and also escorted them one at a time in wrist and leg shackles to the area where they ate. Never was more than one prisoner unshackled from the beds. These were bad hombres, mostly being held for trial by general court martial for killing Aussies. This was the undesired post, but we served our turns in rotation. It was served by two privates and a sergeant. It was great instruction to let you know that was the place to avoid.

The third guard post on the delivery gate was a breeze. One night during my four hours from 8 p.m. to 12 p.m. (2000 to 2400), I had lots of company. There were no deliveries at night and nothing to do except be there, but the top sergeant of the guard was an old Marine legend named Lou Diamond. He had a deep, rasping voice, a goatee, and a big bay window (Southern colloquial for a beer belly). There is no telling what his age might have been, but to my eighteen years he seemed an old, old man. He never seemed to do anything except bellow orders and drink beer. He would sit on a case of Aussie beer, with the case turned up on end, and slowly drink the entire case. On his green blouse, the hash marks and chevrons met. There was also an Aussie Home Guard army soldier there for those four hours and he, too, was an old-timer. The Aussies kept one guard also on the delivery gate, which was probably just to give them something to do. The night was cold and we had a fifty-five gallon drum with the top cut out and three-fourths full of sand. We would pour diesel fuel in the drum and then have a warm flickering fire that would last for hours. A crowd of maybe fifteen Marines not on duty each brought a chair out of our quarters, maybe twenty yards from the delivery gate, and came out to sit around the fire near the delivery gate for a bull session and liar's contest. The old Aussie and Lou Diamond had both been in WWI, and they were having a delightful time telling us kids how easy we had everything compared to them in WWI. Then, they got into an argument about which was roughest, Belleau Wood or Gallipoli, as they were both veterans of these conflicts. I had never heard of Gallipoli, but was curious enough about it to read some information soon after. I remember they nearly came to blows when Lou Diamond, in his rasping voice, told the Aussie, "Gallipoli was a Boy Scout picnic compared to Belleau Wood." We had to physically hold them apart. I recall wishing I had some way to record that conversation along with all of its expletives. In those days, the military service was home to those old-timers and I think the governments just allowed them to stay on in the service if they wanted to.

It was during this guard duty time at the hospital that W.O. and I were walking down a street in downtown Melbourne on our day off and noticed a sign offering Turkish baths for two shillings. We decided to try this as we had never been in one, so in we walked. We followed instructions and took off our clothes and went into a steam room with benches, where the temperature must have been close to boiling. As Marine robot privates accustomed to getting orders for everything, we figured they would tell us when to come out of the steam room, but they didn't; we finally came out just before we would have passed out. I remember standing in an ice-cold shower, looking up at the large brass shower head for about ten minutes, unable to feel anything. Then, we were put on a table and given a massage. We paid our two shillings and left as weak as kittens and decided never to try that idea again; we headed for a pub for refreshment.

After we returned to the Cricket Ground, I went on liberty one afternoon with my cobber, Tex. We rode the tram into downtown Melbourne on Wellington Parade Street and went to the famous pub Young and Jackson's for some refreshment and to say hello to Chloe. I had a pint of beer and Tex had a scotch and water three times while I was enjoying that pint. We left that pub and went to another and repeated the process. Then we left that pub and started to cross one of the main streets when six American sailors from some ship in port were crossing the same street coming toward us. Tex spread his arms and told them to stop right where they were and get back on the other side of the street, because this side of the street belonged to us. He told them if they didn't do it now, that he and his buddy would swab the deck with them. I tried to get an expression on my face that we were mean and bad and loved to fight just for the hell of it. They didn't want any part of Tex and turned and went back across the street. I asked Tex if he was trying to get us killed and his answer was that he could tell which sailors would or would not fight. Needless to say, I let Tex go ahead without me shortly. Why fight unnecessary skirmishes in a long war?

We had been issued green wool uniform jackets that had been made in Australia because they could not get enough green Marine uniform blouses over there to supply the entire division, at that point of time in the war. The jackets later became popular and known as the Eisenhower jacket. Our sea bags were still in New Zealand. We were also issued a new diamond-shaped shoulder patch, designating us as First Marine Division. We were all issued one patch there in the Cricket Ground and I still have that original patch, although the jacket wore out shortly after the war when I was wearing the jacket to Spring Hill College.

Of course, the high command could not let this paradise continue indefinitely, so we were put back into training for the next landing. For our training we were issued new Aussie hobnail high-top shoes and started hiking to our new camp in the small town of Dandenong about twenty miles out of Melbourne. The shoes were heavy and new and stiff and inferior to our suede Marine boondockers, so the troops just took them off, threw them away, and walked in socks. That had been another bad idea, so we were soon issued new American Marine boondockers. In Dandenong, we lived in American pyramid canvas tents with smoky coal stoves in the centers of the tents. The weather turned cold as June 1943 arrived. Much of our training involved hiking and the hikes became longer and longer. For the final hike, they took us out from Dandenong one hundred miles and put us out of the trucks. Each man was given a cloth sack full of uncooked rice (we hated rice) and a cloth sack of raisins, and we were told that all who made it back the one hundred miles to Dandenong in three days would get a three-day pass into Melbourne. There were Marine water trucks along the route to refill canteens, but no other food. There were no towns, no people, no houses, no nothing. Every man in the battalion made it, including our short stocky Lieutenant Colonel Stickney, whom we had nicknamed Mr. Five by Five. We did not have to carry the mortars or machine guns and would ask the rifle companies why they looked so tired and exhausted as we cockily marched along in route step five paces apart. We simply slept on the ground at night; it really was cold, although camp fires were permitted. I slept with my cobber Don Sullivan back to back. We did not pitch our pup tent, but dug a large foxhole at night and slept in the hole. Together we had two shelter halves, two ponchos, four blankets, and slept in our dungarees and an army field jacket we had been issued. After the first night, most of the platoon copied Sully's and my idea of sleeping in a hole with a cobber. This was great training for the coming tropical jungle rainforest campaign.

I recall one event at Dandenong that must be recorded. One afternoon, about ten of us from the mortar platoon in two trucks went the few miles from our tent camp into downtown Dandenong to unload coal (charcoal briquets) from their small narrow-gauge railroad cars. At that time, Dandenong looked about like Dodge City in *Gunsmoke* films. There was a pub across from the railroad yard and our sergeant got a commitment of obedience and silence from all hands, then took me with him across the street to the pub for a large imperial quart-sized bottle of Melbourne Bitter. The old sergeant bought one and only one for each man. As I recall they cost one and six, but he collected two shillings from each man and pocketed the change. When we entered the small pub, there was a pretty blond Aussie girl sitting there having a pint while breastfeeding her baby. She was completely topless, which seemed to be the custom, and as large as Dolly Parton. She greeted us in a friendly manner and told us "the little yawnkee barstard's father" was an American sailor from the cruiser *Quincy*. She only knew the father's first name and reported it was the generic sailor name of Jack. I remember thinking "Jack" was probably dead in the Battle of Savo. She then began to tell us how "no good" American sailors were and was astonished when we agreed with her fully. The sergeant then told her most American sailors were recruited from prisons in America and had to have Marines aboard ships to guard them and make them obey orders. He got her home address and promised to be back and see her later. We carried our bottles of beer in a large burlap sack back across to the train yard and every man opened his bottle with his belt buckle. We unloaded the coal in record time and rode back to camp sitting on top of the coal singing, "Bless 'Em All" and "When This War Is Over We Will All Enlist Again" not feeling the cold wind at all.

Deacon came down hard on Sullivan and me and gave us

another of his famous lengthy lectures about depravity. "Sully" was another of my good friends, who had been transferred into our squad from Headquarters Company on Guadalcanal. I recall Sully loved to get a pint of vanilla ice cream from the PX in Dandenong and warm it on the stove in the tent until it nearly melted. Then he would drink it from the round cardboard carton.

Tex was always in trouble of some sort and frequently confined to camp on weekends in Dandenong. One weekend, we were all in Melbourne on liberty, while Tex remained in Dandenong confined to camp. He found out a brand-new second lieutenant was officer of the day. Tex put on his uniform, went over to the company office, and told the lieutenant he was back from a detail and ready to pick up his pass. He told the lieutenant the first sergeant had said he would leave it on his desk. The lieutenant naturally couldn't find the nonexistent pass and obligingly made out (another) one for fast-talking Tex. Tex boarded the first electric train and rode toward Melbourne. He said about halfway there he got off at some obscure tiny suburb and went into the closest pub for some refreshment. There at the bar sat our first sergeant Francis P. McGrath, who collared him and took him back to camp and the brig. At a reunion many years after the war, our first sergeant told me he really didn't remember me at all, but he surely remembered Tex. In the final years of the first sergeant's life, he and Tex were nearly constantly on the telephone, the closest of friends.

Tex told us we clowns were going to be out there until we were all dead, but he was going to keep going to sick call and whine about the pain in his fingers and get sent back to the states. He accomplished this but they found he was OK and put him into the 26th Marines in the Fourth Marine Division and he landed in the first wave on Iwo Jima and after several weeks was wounded and evacuated.

One afternoon, W.O. and I were walking along in downtown Melbourne and noticed a Marine out in the middle of the street—it was Sullivan. Sully had stopped a car and was arguing with the driver and a Bobby (policeman), who had on the classic black pith helmet and uniform with shiny silver buttons. The Aussies had no gasoline and powered their cars with coal gas obtained by pulling a little trailer behind the car that had a small stove-type contraption in the trailer and a fire burning in the stove, producing a gas vapor piped into the car engine that would move the car along at about fifteen miles per hour. Sullivan was blind drunk and had stopped the car so he could barbecue a dead pigeon he had found in the street. The Bobby was putting in a call for the MPs when I arrived and I assured the Bobby that Sully meant no harm, that I would see that he stayed out of trouble. I asked Sully if he wanted to go back to the Cricket Ground and he replied, "No," that his girl was expecting him. He knew which tram to catch, so I went with him and W.O. went elsewhere.

We were standing on the crowded tram holding the hanging straps when Sully suddenly began swearing in a most vile manner. The tram was full of ladies and I began to apologize for his language and pass out his cigarettes when he said, "There's our corner!" He just stepped off the tram while we were doing about twenty-five miles per hour. It was an open tram car with no doors. I looked back and Sully was rolling head over heels in the cinders. I pulled the stop cord, got off, ran back, and found he was okay, except for some bad abrasions and torn pants and jacket. It had been the right corner and he guided us to his girlfriend's house. The girl's mother helped her daughter clean Sully's wounds and he went to sleep on the sofa. I entertained myself with their wind-up player piano until all was quiet and I was satisfied Sully would be asleep for a long time; I left then to find the tram back into the downtown center of Melbourne, where all of the action seemed to always be going on.

16

That strange feeling of power came over me as I was part of that long, lean, green machine going through the streets of Melbourne.

It is not possible to leave Melbourne quite yet with so much still in the memory bank. A few more pages should be sufficient.

Soon after our replacements came in and much of the sickness had subsided, the First Marine Division held a parade through the streets of Melbourne. We (the First Regiment) assembled by battalions right outside the Cricket Ground early one clear, cool morning; when the regiment was in place, the band played the "Star Spangled Banner" and ran up the colors—a huge American flag—on a gigantic flagstaff. There was just enough wind to make it stand out and flap loosely. I am still likely to recall that scene at a football game today and choke up a little bit. Ransom, as usual, came to everyone's rescue by remarking in a loud voice how "that wind burns your eyes and makes them water." An Australian Navy band appeared from somewhere and joined in at the head of H Company blaring out "Waltzing Matilda" as we marched several blocks to join the rest of the Division. Then, the First Marine Division band led off the whole parade playing "Semper Fidelis," followed by "Onward Christian Soldiers" set to march time.

As an old Murphy High School Band snare drummer, I noticed all snare drum cadences and still remember the unusual cadence the Australian band used, as I had never heard it before. It was "purr rum, purr rump tump, oomp tum tum, purr rum tum tiddy tiddy oomp tum tum, purr rum, purr rump tump oomp tum tum, tiddy tiddy oomp tum tum, clang" (cymbals), then repeated over and over. I remember the bass drum seemed to have a leopard skin draped over it. Isn't it strange how that cadence and scene are burned into my memory from so long ago?

That strange feeling of power came over me as I was part of that long, lean, green machine going through the streets of

Melbourne—every man in step, head up, shoulders back, many thousands of miles from home, on foreign soil. That damn comedian Ransom mumbled in a low voice, "Uncle Sam's Marines are showing off." I had a feeling part of the U.S.A. is right here, with nearly every state represented around me.

It would not be possible to omit mentioning the Australian Women's Army Service with the women's smart uniforms and A.W.A.S. insignia. Some Marine comic almost immediately named them the "always willing after sunset girls."

Probably during the first week we were in Melbourne, Deacon told me he had a blind date for me and that I had to help him because she was the sister of his girlfriend; he had been told by their mother, it was both sisters dating together or none at all. Deacon assured me he had seen the sister and added "YOU'LL NOT BE SOR-REE!" We met the girls downtown, and Shirley was as pretty as Elizabeth Taylor. We took them to eat in a really nice restaurant to try to impress them, and then to the movies, where we, of course, sat in the dress circle, and then to St. Kilda, which was a Coney Island–type of amusement park. When we took the girls home on the electric train, we met their mother, Tuppie, and their grandmother, Nana.

Tuppie then took Deacon and me aside, read us her "articles of war" and made us agree to abide by the articles. These were nice girls and remained nice girls, but that was due to

165

their training and Tuppie's "articles of war," not our sterling personalities. Shirley's father had been dead for a number of years, having died when she was a little girl from the effects of mustard gas in WWI. These four lovely ladies lived in a very modest little house in the suburb of Glenferrie and we would repeatedly visit them as our family in Australia, always leaving in time to catch the last midnight train back to the Cricket Ground. I enjoyed taking Shirley through the streets of Melbourne for all the Marines to see and gawk as I went by with her on my arm. Shirley was sixteen and I was now eighteen. The old men would shout, "Give 'er a go, Yank, she's over aighteen!" Deacon and I would take the girls out maybe twice a week and take Tuppie, too, for something like the movie *Gone With the Wind*. Today, Shirley is my daughter's mother-in-law, but to add the rest of that story right now would not be strictly a memory of WWII.

Deacon and I enjoyed cooking a full meal for the girls and acting as chefs; since there was no food rationing except for tea, the sky was the limit! We enjoyed this immensely usually cooking gigantic steaks and would do it frequently to prevent being a burden and expense to the girls. We would bring the raw materials and do the cooking, wearing aprons. Their civilian clothing was rationed and gasoline seemed to be non-existent.

Another thing that should be mentioned is the return to

Melbourne of the Australian Army Ninth Division. It seems to me we had been there several months when this occurred. I suppose Great Britain had sent them home from North Africa as soon as ships were available, because Australia was so un-protected from Japan. Most of the Australian and New Zea-land troops had been sent to fight Hitler long before the Pearl Harbor attack. The Ninth Division troops were veterans of the North Africa campaign who had fought Rommel, and resented the presence of the First Marine Division in Melbourne. We made much more money than they did and there were lots of fights and even riots. We could show the girls a better time then they could. The Marines learned we were safe in twos but vulnerable alone, because the Diggers would jump you as a gang. Finally, to stop this, the First Division hosted a beer party in the Cricket Ground and both divisions got drunk to-gether. This seemed to defuse the situation. The Fifth and Sev-enth and Eleventh Marines came to the Cricket Grounds and joined us. I remember clearly, the beer was brought in large wooden kegs in wagons pulled by Clydesdales, just as in the Budweiser ads, but only two horses to each wagon.

I recall leaving Shirley's one night in time to catch the last (midnight) train. I was alone without Deacon that night. This was before the beer party and when the situation was most strained. As I approached the train station in Glenferrie, it was necessary to pass through a dimly lighted tunnel, maybe thirty yards long, and up an inside flight of stairs that led to the train platform above at the station depot. I entered the tunnel, felt uneasy, and backed out of the tunnel to the last house before the tunnel. Here I picked up a brick from the flower bed border in the front yard, broke it in half on the curbing, and entered the tunnel with the brick halves held up and ready for action. Of course, there was nothing in the tunnel, so I, with a foolish feeling, and happy there were no witnesses, deposited the brick bats in a trash can on the station platform as the last train swished up to the station. I saw a Marine alone in one of the compartments, so I walked to that door and entered. It was obvious he was glad to see me as two Marines make an expedition, so we relaxed and traveled together to Flinder's Street Station, changed trains for Richmond, debarked, and walked into the Cricket Ground, telling lies and making small talk.

Our training intensified, so we went aboard an Australian Navy troop training ship for night ship-to-shore landings. It was the same old boring training for all of us old-timers except for one thing: We slept in hammocks, British style; there were no bunks. It took us several nights to completely master the hammocks. Getting in without dumping seemed to be the problem. We were issued more of the despised C-rations, but with a slight twist. These had been canned in Australia with the same wholesome ingredients in the same proportions used, giving them the identical taste. The canned round crackers contained the same ingredients and had the same taste, but with one exception. The powdered coffee in a little flat can was there, as usual, but with a real honest-to-goodness **T.S.** (meaning Tough S——t) slip stating the manufacturer must apologize for the inclusion of coffee due to the tea shortage. We loved having the genuine T.S. slips and used them for poker chips; we also passed them out to one another whenever anyone had a gripe or complaint. Each little slip of paper had a capital T.S. printed at the top.

Finally, the sad day arrived for our departure; we boarded American liberty ships with insufficient bunks and no heads. We had been in Australia nine months. Most of us just slept on the open steel deck, which we preferred. We had never been issued mattresses the entire time in Australia, although we did have U.S. canvas cots in our Dandenong camp; my point is, we had never been allowed to become soft and civilized.

The heads on the liberty ships were built on the deck out of new lumber and extended over the edge of the deck; everything simply fell directly into the ocean, seemingly no concern for submarines as we stayed inside the Great Barrier Reef in relatively shallow water. Submarines do not like shallow water. We had been told we were now under the command of the U.S. Army and had been transferred to MacArthur's jurisdiction. We howled and barked and called one another "doggies." We felt we had been deserted by the U.S. Navy. Round Army fatigue hats were issued and immediately thrown away. As we left the docks in Melbourne, hundreds of girls gathered to see us depart; the Marines inflated hundreds of condoms and let them drift back in to the shore. I recall this embarrassed even me. For many months, mail to and from Australia exceeded mail to the U.S. We traveled north through some beautiful small islands of the Great Barrier Reef for many boring days, cursing the liberty ships and Douglas MacArthur as the cause of our cramped quarters. We ate mostly the despised cold C-rations out of cans with our trusty spoons, and collected more T.S. slips. Between leaving Melbourne, riding those liberty ships, and being told we were under army command, I expect our morale could not have been any lower. We hated everybody and everything except one another, which might have been what our high command was trying to accomplish.

We arrived at a large island off the coast of New Guinea named Goodenough Island. One can only imagine what a regiment of Marines did with that name. On Goodenough, we went many miles, in trucks, perhaps fifteen from the docks, and made tent camps for more training. Goodenough was actually a beautiful island with mountains that seemed to touch the sky. Much of the island was cultivated and clear of jungle. The best thing on Goodenough was a mountain stream within a city block of our camp where clear, cold water poured into a small boulder-lined natural swimming hole that was about one-half the size of a basketball court. We could swim or wash our clothes every minute that we had free. I remember this stream came down from a mountain that was so high the top was hidden by clouds clustered perpetually around the summit. I am not sure we ever saw the top of that mountain.

Our training on Goodenough consisted mostly of more long, long hikes. On one of these long hikes we were returning to our camp and paused for a ten-minute break. An old Yankee friend reminded me of this at a company reunion a few years ago. We were sitting there telling lies when I shouted, jumped to my feet, and ran off waving a machete. I had spotted sugar cane growing in a field close by and came back with a half-dozen stalks, distributing them to all the Southern boys. We taught the Yankees to peal the cane and cut it into chewable-sized pieces; we soon had the whole platoon, including the officers, chewing sugar cane. The Yankees thought we were brilliant. We finished the last few miles to camp singing ribald songs, all hyper on sugar-cane juice.

It was also in this Goodenough camp location that we were building a deluxe head in the rocky soil and using dynamite to make the digging easier. One charge was too heavy and a large piece of rock came down through a tent and killed Jontiff. He was the Marine who had the roll of wire break his arm on the Fiji practice landing before Guadalcanal. Jontiff used to jokingly proclaim that all of us clowns would be eventually killed in the war and he would be the only survivor in the platoon, and, just to let us know how much he missed us, he would p--s on our graves. The "dynamite head" was a structural masterpiece and included a new lumber, boxed-in affair like a coffin, complete with rifle sling leather-hinged lids for the "four-holer" to reduce fly activity and had handles on each end like a stretcher, so it could be periodically lifted aside by four good men and the ritual performed of pouring in a gasoline and diesel mixture to burn the contents. After one of these burning procedures, the contraption had been replaced and unsuspected fumes accumulated under the box. A member of our platoon named Fisher was the first to use the head after the burning; he sat on it, lit a cigarette, and dropped the match inside. The resulting explosion was considerable. The hilarity was out of control as the not-seriously-injured Marine was carried to the sick bay tent in the knee-chest position, sans pants and pubic hair, on a canvas stretcher by four laughing cobbers. No sympathy. No loving-kindness. No kind words of consolation.

We were introduced to LSTs on Goodenough and made several practice landings on nearby islands. I remember we made one landing complete with Sherman tanks and moved inland in the prescribed manner, only to come up on a native village and find the natives were all nine-tenths white and the women all dressed only in grass skirts. They all came to smilingly gawk at us and we were delightedly gawking at them when our officers proceeded to get us off that island faster than we had come ashore. One Marine comic remarked, "There must have been some very active missionaries on this island; we finally find Dorothy Lamour and they take us away!"

This next little story is about the value of discipline. While on Goodenough, we went on many all-night working parties loading and unloading cargo. One night we arrived at the docks by truck with the canvas cover off the back of the truck. We were sitting on the bench seats in the back of the truck, telling lies. We had driven to the docks from our distant tent camp and pulled up on the docks beside a ship. One standing Marine on our truck looked up and shouted: "Get off the truck now, jump!" Everybody obeyed due to discipline, and a giant life raft on a rail slide rumbled down the slide off the ship and landed on the truck right where we had been sitting and crushed it. We never solved the mystery of who tripped the mechanism to cause that near fatal accident but we knew it had been deliberately tripped. There were no injuries but just by inches. It was not an American ship.

Another event that occurred on Goodenough worth recalling was an entertainment program put on by our regimental band. The highlight of the nonsense in the 1943 program was a song composed and sung by the band dressed in ridiculous zoot suit costumes they had made. I was stationed with a member of the band later in the war at Boca Chica NAS, Florida. His name was Bill Newell and he recalled the words one afternoon while I wrote them down. Any complaining or verbal griping in the Marine Corps was referred to as "beating your gums," hence the title of the song.

BEAT EM
'Twas in boot camp in forty-two
DIs were tough and horse s———, too
Know your rifle, get good scores
Bull's-eyes? I got Maggie's drawers
It's humiliating—

Chorus:

Beat 'em, everybody beat 'em
Yes beat 'em. Till your gums get sore
Oh beat 'em, everybody beat 'em
Yes, beat 'em, till your gums get sore
Maneuvers, problems every day
Rugged hikes, 'twas hell to pay
Standing guard every other night
Damn it, we joined up to fight
We did

Chorus

They broke out the band and fell us out
The rear echelon began to shout

Where to, Bud? Don't know, Pal
Don't worry, Mac; I'll watch your gal
He did

Chorus

Our trip across was one big flop
Quarters were cramped, chow was slop
Sweeping, swabbing, cleaning decks
When we hit shore, we were hell of a wrecks
It's murder

Chorus

Move that gear from ship to shore
Damn it, Sarge, my back is sore
There ain't no justice in this Corps
Tough s———, Mac, just blame the war
It's all f———d up

Chorus

Shellings, bombings all the time
Digging foxholes in the slime
Out of those holes the corporal said

To hell with you Joe, conditions red
Here they come

Chorus

The Army is here, we're leaving now
No more of this damn Guadalcanal
First-class girls, grub and wine
Dates and parties all the time—Whoopie
Oh, yeah

Chorus

Melbourne, malaria, nurses fair . . .
Hospital time, we've done our share
Now, here on Goodenough we sit
Ready to go through the same old s———
I asked for it—You got it
Semper Fidelis

Chorus

We figured the high command could not be happy with
our beautiful swimming hole, so we left Goodenough on LSTs
so packed with supplies and equipment and ammunition that

we just rode and slept wherever we could, under vehicles, on tanks, on piles of boxes, just anywhere. War for the common private is mostly standing in line, performing endless boring senseless tasks and hard work, telling lies, and trying to make the best of thousands of bad situations.

We went north to New Guinea and went to Lae, Finchaven, and Salamoa, but I don't remember in what order. I recall more long hikes and crossing jungle streams with my carbine and my mortar bipod held high over my head, the water chest-deep, feeling security in that there was more than just me for a crocodile's lunch. We were issued new jungle hammocks, which kept us off the ground at night, and had a built-in mosquito net that opened with a five-foot zipper. The hammock had a waterproof roof to which the netting was attached. The hammocks were practical and much appreciated by the troops.

On one of our long hikes, we stopped late one afternoon for chow and to sleep, hanging our hammocks from trees in the jungle swamp. The chow truck met our battalion at a pre-arranged meeting place. Benny managed to get a box of cigars of a brand called Habanello and gave each of us one as a special treat. I decided to just stick mine in my mouth, walk around with it, chew on it a little, and talk and act tough. I soon became sick and could not stand up; I sat in the jungle while the platoon went several hundred yards to eat. I remember sitting there alone in that semi-swamp and seeing fish about five inches long come out of the water and walk around on their fins. It's a wonder I wasn't convinced that biological evolution might be a reasonable idea.

Deacon told me how to handle tobacco, just put a tiny piece in my mouth every day and simply suck it. I was soon able to stuff my mouth with Beechnut Chewing Tobacco and act as idiotic as anyone else.

We celebrated Christmas Day with an extremely rare turkey dinner that always included ten pieces of mixed hard candy and then went aboard a LCI for the short trip, overnight, over to Cape Gloucester, New Britain.

Before we left New Guinea, our second battalion received a new commanding officer named Lieutenant Colonel James Masters. He was fresh from the U.S. and seemed to be a good man, except for being a little green in the field. He assembled the battalion, gave us a pep talk on New Guinea, and told us in the coming campaign he wanted us to "kill the bastards" whenever we could. Someone reported he had lost a brother on Wake Island. After his talk, Ransom always referred to us as "Masters' Bastards." Colonel Masters was the same height as my father and had the exact same colored blue eyes. I liked the man immediately; he hated the Japanese just like the rest of us.

17

Due to the gloomy weather, almost everything about the campaign of Cape Gloucester is recorded in my memory bank in black and white . . .

========

The high command landed the whole division at the Cape at the western tip of New Britain, but landed our battalion about eight miles east, down the coast, at the foot of a mountain called Mt. Tuali. Our objective was to close the jungle coastal trail that ran along the foot of the mountain that seemed to touch the sky. The idea was the Japs at the airport would be prevented from retreating up the coast toward Rabaul. If anyone is interested in any of this ancient history, you need to look at what I am talking about with a map in hand. There were two small native villages called Sag Sag and Tuali on the map, and that's about where we were. My guess is this area of the world contains the thickest jungle in existence.

After the usual naval bombardment of the beach area, our LCI came in to the beach through a break in the coral reef; the Navy put us ashore on a black sand beach with the rainforest jungle coming down to within twenty feet of the water. I might add there was always some comedian who claimed to know the exact cost of every round of naval gunfire or bomb dropped and, when the bombardment began, he would urge Uncle Sam to spend another specified amount, e.g., $175 or $325, and not to be thrifty. Our landing was the day after Christmas and our attitude was, "Let's get on with the program, because the sooner we do, the sooner we can go home and end this miserable war!" The landing craft infantry (LCI) that we rode over from New Guinea was the only time I'd ever gone aboard one of those craft. It put us up almost on the beach and we had to wade through only knee-deep water to come ashore. I came down the starboard ramp. The Navy ran the big LSTs through the coral break also and we soon were unloading them into the jungle as mass organized confusion, as we called it. The Japs had a brand-new 20mm gun mounted there on our landing beach that had not quite been made serviceable. The ammunition for it was still in a stack of wooden boxes and not yet in

180

magazines. We naturally broke open one of the ammo boxes and found each 20mm shell individually wrapped in a sort of tissue paper with Jap writing all over each sheet. We would have enjoyed firing it if we could find a magazine, but I suppose the Japs took off with the magazines. If there had been any Japs on the beach before we landed, they had taken off into the jungle from the naval shelling. Everything was unloaded from our vessels and crowded into the jungle.

The native coastal trail we were to block was nothing more than a single-file footpath, but our battalion went to work and fortified a semicircle from the beach inward that took in an area I would estimate to be approximately three city blocks. When we were still in New Guinea, we had made hundreds of circular barbed wire contraptions that were coiled and then could be uncoiled to form a rapid defensive perimeter. They were named concertinos, and were quickly set up, then additional barbed wire aprons added. We did all the barbed wire work without gloves and I think some new swear words may have been invented. Our 81mm mortar battery was located in the center of the semicircle about fifty yards inland from the beach.

As we came ashore, the monsoon season began and the rain started and continued as long as we were there. Never have men endured such relentless rain. We were grateful for even a few hours without rain. Due to the gloomy weather, almost everything about the campaign of Cape Gloucester is recorded in my memory bank in black and white, almost nothing in color. A 75mm battery from the 11th Marines was attached to our battalion, but they could never get a field of fire due to the dense jungle and never fired a round. They were very close to us and we kidded them relentlessly about being used as lowly riflemen, stevedores, and ammunition carriers for our mortars.

Now that we were under Army command, our field rations changed to something called K-rations. They came in brown waxed cardboard boxes about twice the size of a box of Cracker Jacks. At first, we were pleased with the change, but the K-rations soon all tasted the same, and we loathed them, too.

Firing a mortar in a jungle is like throwing rocks at the enemy from inside of a barn, and throwing through holes in the roof. The Japs hit our lines one dark night during a wild howling monsoon lightning, thunder, and rainstorm. The one-cell flashlights we had been issued on Goodenough were definitely not good enough, and mine was the only one that would work. They had issued one flashlight to each gun squad and the gunner was designated to carry it and keep it dry and working. They used one D battery and were turned on and off by twisting it from both ends at the same time Using the range card and staying above a 75-degree elevation for mass clearance, we answered our O.P. directed fire orders and brought our bursts in to fifteen yards of our lines. We used H.E. light only; this was very unnerving because we were firing over our own buddies, but we followed the range card precisely and leveled bubbles before every round so as to place each round exactly where we were directed. Opening the canisters and getting the correct number of increments on each shell had to be done in the dark by feeling, or in the flashes of the wild lightning as the storm raged through the whole fight of several hours. Gunfire and thunder were mixed and confusing. The next morning, we had to dig up our mortar base plate because it had settled so deep in the mud. Colonel Masters came to our squad the next morning and commended us highly; he wanted to see the one-cell flashlight. He asked us our names and remembered mine; he would call me Phillips whenever he saw me. I figured he associated my name with somebody he already knew.

The fire fight was all over at daylight and our mortar platoon was very close to our surgical tent. All the wounded were brought in on stretchers, with the stretcher bearers staggering and slipping and falling repeatedly in the deep mud and relentless rain. We knew most of the wounded, with some of them from our platoon who had been on our O.P. It was that morning that I decided I wanted to study medicine, because of the helpless feeling of seeing all the wounded and not having a clue as to how to help them.

Collecting the debris the next morning, we noted many of the yellow range cards packed in the canisters had been kissed by girls in the ammunition factory, leaving red lipstick imprints on the cards and maybe a name written in lipstick with a message like, "Love you, Betty!" These cards were prized and passed around in the rain for every one to kiss the red lip imprints and make obscene remarks to Betty. Betty or Marie or Ruth never knew how much we appreciated those range cards.

The surf here on our little beach was, at times, tremendous where there was the break in the coral reef; one of the Navy doctors and I loved to swim in it and ride the waves. His home was on the Atlantic and we both understood how to let the undertow carry us out, then go to the bottom and push up. We sort of watched out for each other. Most of the guys didn't feel it safe to swim there. We swam in our shorts then, but on Cape Gloucester we soon threw our underclothes and socks away and simply lived in our herringbone dungarees, boondockers, and helmet, just as we had done on Guadalcanal.

One day, artillery or mortar shells began to land just off the beach and we raced to our mortars. The O.P. soon gave us an azimuth and range and we fired white phosphorus for spotting. The O.P. corrected range and deflection orders and then ordered ten rounds from all guns as concentrated fire. Benny was in charge of the O.P. We sent the forty rounds on their way, and no more came in. Ransom surmised that Tojo now knew he had come up with a bad idea. We collected a few more range cards with lipstick imprints and messages.

When it was determined that most of the Cape Gloucester Japs had retreated around the north side of Mt. Tuali, our battalion was ordered west to join the rest of the division at the Cape. We visited our small cemetery on the side of that mountain (where a Marine combat photographer caught me in a group picture that appeared in the *VFW* magazine a few years ago), and then we started on foot to the Cape. The artillery battery had to be moved by landing craft.

The coastal trail to the Cape became a mud hole miles long and I recall slipping and cursing my way along in single file carrying a full pack and forty-six-pound mortar bipod, when I suddenly came face-to-face with Colonel Masters about halfway to the Cape. He was just standing there watching the battalion go by. He asked, "Phillips, are you tired?" I answered "No, sir," and he retorted "You look tired to me." So, he called a ten-minute break. I remember thinking, he calls a ten-minute break because one of his privates looks tired? As soon as I sat down, someone shouted, "Come look at what I have found," and no more than twenty yards from where we were, was a perfectly camouflaged seaplane hangar, complete with inside dock, gasoline drums, an extra propeller, tools, etc.! The place gave me the creeps, so I slipped a round into the chamber of my carbine as I walked around the dock in the dim light. Colonel Masters thought it a good idea; he took out his pistol and did the same, as did all the other Marines in there. We knew we had found one of Washing Machine Charlie's home ports.

I must mention that we were trudging along a jungle road in the rain a few days later and saw a Marine bulldozer go down and disappear in the mud. It was a slow process, but someone threw a line to the driver and hauled him to safety across a pond of mud as the seat and, finally, the exhaust stack slowly sank out of sight, with the engine running and the tracks turning. I bet that thing is resting there today, no telling how deep down in that bottomless jungle.

After we arrived at the Cape, we were moved about from place to place, always working in the deep jungle and always going by foot. It was difficult for any vehicle to move in that vast sea of mud. There seemed to be few landmarks except things like Hill 660 or a group of wrecked Jap landing craft on the beach. It would be impossible to ever go back there and find any place we had been except our initial landing place. I will wager no one has ever returned to that battle site or any-where on Cape Gloucester except to move the cemetery. The place remains in my memory as the land of dismal gloom and mud.

Several things are in my memory, though, that I must re-cord. One was a jungle location that W.O. and I found when we went exploring from one of our camps into the deep jungle. It was not more than five hundred yards away, down a trail in the gloom. It was a Jap hospital tent about ten by twenty yards in size, abandoned, dead Jap soldiers in uniform on canvas stretchers in line on the deck, maybe a total of twenty, all re-duced to skeletons; no odor except the strange odor like Col-gate tooth powder. There was a large folding table containing a beautiful binocular microscope, scattered glass syringes, surgical instruments, ampoules, pans, basins, bandages, etc. The scene was weird and eerie to say the least. All of the dead Japs still had on wrapped leggings.

On another roaming expedition, W.O., Sullivan, and I, maybe two miles from another of our camps in deep jungle, found an abandoned Jap supply dump with stacked boxes everywhere about the size of a baseball diamond infield. No trees had been cut down; everything had been neatly stacked among the trees. We opened a big green wooden case and took out a Jap machine gun that could be carried like a stretcher with the four handles. It fired strip brass ammunition; we opened a case of this and fired the thing until it nearly melted as it became so hot and finally locked tight in its own cloud of steam. Sully wanted to try to blow up the whole dump, but we convinced him that might not be a good idea as we might blow up with it. There is no way to describe the density of that jungle unless you were there. Some of the banyan trees were so large that one tree would cover an area as large as a half of a football field and another person could be a few feet away and entirely hidden.

It was in this position that W.O. met a Navy photographer looking for Marines from the same hometown and W.O. came to get me so we could have our picture taken by the photographer. He said he would send it to our hometown newspaper. For the picture, we changed clothes from our nasty dungarees into khakis that we had in our packs. The photographer gave us each a print several days later, but nothing ever appeared in our paper or our families would have seen it.

One calm night, for no apparent reason, a gigantic dead tree trunk, perhaps ten feet in diameter and fifty feet tall, fell over in our camp area, killing Don Rouse from Biloxi and breaking both legs of another man in our company. I was sleeping in another tent about twenty feet from Don. The whole company (about three hundred men) turned out with Coleman lights from the galley to lift the tree and retrieve his flattened body. This happened numerous times in the division while we were at Cape Gloucester.

Benny chose me to go through Don's personal effects with him because Don had been a good friend of mine. Don had been in the intelligence section of our company and had a propaganda sheet in his pack that had been dropped on us on New Guinea. Benny already had one, so he told me to take it because we could not send it home to his family. The Japs had dropped it on us thinking we were Australian troops; it says, "Take your sweet time at the front, Aussie. I got my hands full right now with your sweet tootsie at home." The leaflet shows a slick-looking Marine with greased hair and a tiny mustache as he cavorts with an Australian girl while an Australian soldier chases a far less attractive native girl. It has to be the single funniest thing of WWII. When they were dropped, none actually landed on our company, but we all knew about

it from other units in the division. We had one man in our platoon with a mustache and, after this, he had the nickname of
"Slick."

The next day, a team of Seabees came to our area and cut
down all of the trees with a precision that amazed us. The man
in charge was from Oregon, and he could drop a tree with the
accuracy of a genius. No tents were moved; he simply dropped
the trees between the tents. This was the first time I had ever
seen a chainsaw, and it was carried by two men. It had handles
like a stretcher and we simply gawked at their skill. The giant
logs were cut into sections and we rolled and carried them
away.

As we were preparing to leave Cape Gloucester, Lucas
and I were put on an all-night working party to load vehicles
aboard ship. The sea was rough, and the large landing craft (we
called them tank lighters as they were large enough to carry a
tank) we were on came alongside the ship to transfer the two
vehicles aboard. We had control of the air and sea in the area
and the ship had rigged bright floodlights along the starboard
side. There were some Army soldiers in the working party
with us who were part of the force that was relieving us. We
would take a load of Army stuff ashore and come back with a
load of Marine gear to go aboard. These were our worn-out
vehicles going aboard. The Army boys had not had the tremendous experience in loading ships that we had had, and in plac-
ing a lifting cable under the bumper hooks, a soldier stood in

front of the truck to place the cable instead of to the side. The sea was rough; the truck shifted due to a huge wave and pinned the soldier to the bulkhead in the rear of the tank lighter. Lucas jumped into the cab and tried to start the truck engine, while I assured the soldier we would be successful. The truck engine would not start and the battery was too weak to back the truck without starting, as it would have had to back slightly uphill in the landing craft. The soldier was looking me in the eye and begging us to help him as the truck was crushing him slowly. We unhooked the cables from the front bumper and left the cables attached to the rear bumper. Then the coxswain backed away from the ship until the strain on the rear bumper cables moved the truck away from him about a foot or two. We lifted him up onto the little deck on the rear of the landing craft and, then, the tank lighter came alongside of the ship. The ship let down some gangway stairs with a small platform at the bottom, and a wire stretcher was brought down by some sailors and passed to us. We placed the soldier on the stretcher and strapped him in, then passed the stretcher to the sailors on the platform in a wild procedure with the lighter rising and falling ten feet with each wave. We nearly lost the soldier overboard, but the Lord gave us a ten-second interval of small waves, and we successfully passed the stretcher to the sailors on the platform. An Army major came down as we were transferring the two vehicles and commended us for the whole procedure. He had been an eyewitness to the tragedy; he said the soldier had two broken legs, but would be OK. Lucas commented to me that we were lucky because, had Benny been that officer, he would have torn us up for not having a line on that stretcher when we passed it.

I must not fail to tell of a few events that happened before we left Cape Gloucester. We were camped in one of those deep dense jungle areas, eating breakfast and standing in the usual continuous downpour. Breakfast was oatmeal and coffee and we were using an upended fifty-five-gallon drum for a table outside of the galley tent. Suddenly, Colonel Masters appeared with his mess kit full of oatmeal and asked to share our table. As he spoke, his coffee cup dumped; I showed him how to keep his thumb on the little gizmo to prevent that from happening. He thanked me and asked if we would keep someone from stealing his oatmeal while he got some more coffee. He had a great sense of humor.

Probably about a month before we left the Cape, we were camped in a dense jungle, and Les Clark and I were scheduled to stand the midnight-to-four watch. This was a platoon guard post and was simply a telephone watch in the jungle. It was pitch-black dark, and we simply sat by the field telephone and fed the mosquitoes. Suddenly, the telephone rang—it was our battalion headquarters telling us we had night fighters in the air and if they called a condition red (air-raid alert), they would call and let us know. Soon, the drone of an aircraft overhead made Clark and me both remark that it really did sound like

Washing Machine Charlie, but we relaxed and waited for the phone to ring. It was Charlie and he dropped one bomb almost in our pocket. No one was hit, but Benny nearly destroyed his precious hammock coming out through the netting. At roll call the next morning, Clark and I were told by Benny that we were on permanent mess duty forever and ever. Benny did not want or accept any explanations from us. He felt we were old-timers and should have known that was Charlie. He was right and we did not argue.

Les and I gathered our belongings in a downpour, and trudged to the battalion mess tent, about two hundred yards away. The tent was close to a stream about twelve feet wide and two feet deep, with clear water and a sandy bottom. All of the best trees had been taken for stringing hammocks, so we strung ours on a ridge maybe twenty feet high, and thirty yards away from the mess tent. Japs were no longer a problem.

We were given the lowest job of pot walloping; we would simply take the large pots into the stream and clean them with rags and sand. It really wasn't hard work. Since everyone was soaked all day every day, at night we would hang our clothes on our hammock strings. We would sleep in the nude in our hammocks, wrapped in our trusty blankets, maybe hugging our weapons. You needed the blanket in the night. It rained twelve inches in three hours that night in the "mother of all rainstorms," and the little stream turned into a roaring river. The cooks and mess men down by the mess tent suddenly found themselves suspended in their hammocks in rapidly rising water in pitch-black dark. All they could do was unzip their hammocks and climb the trees the hammocks were tied to, in the nude. Clark and I awoke at daylight to look down on all these naked, shivering Marines clinging to the trunks and sitting on the limbs of trees. We dissolved in fits of laughter. Their hammocks were shreds, their clothes were gone, and their weapons were gone. The mess tent, stoves, pots, and cases of food were gone, but Clark and I were high and safe and crying in delight. No sympathy, no kind words of consolation. Everything was gradually recovered during the next two days by following the stream after it returned to normal. We brought back the pots and stoves, etc. Labels were missing from the cans of food, so there was a large pot for meat, one for vegetables, and one for fruit. Recovered mystery content cans were opened, so a stew of meat, a stew of vegetables, and a stew of fruit were served. The troops said it was the best chow our cooks had ever prepared and suggested they continue the process from now on. There was always undaunted humor and nonsense.

18

"I think the Marine Corps has forgotten
where Pavuvu is," one man said.
"I think God has forgotten where
Pavuvu is," came a reply.
"God couldn't forget because
he made everything."
"Then I bet he wishes he could
forget he made Pavuvu."

====

We left Cape Gloucester after having been there several
months, but I cannot remember if we went by troop ship or
LST, probably by ship. The constant scuttlebutt we had per-

petuated was that we would be returning to Melbourne and the glorious girls, bountiful beer, and fabulous food. We were disgusted to unload in the Russell Island group at a place called Pavuvu. This was supposed to be a rest camp. It was an uninhabited island now with an abandoned coconut plantation. It was totally primitive, practically next door to Guadalcanal. We had been put into another massive, monstrous, mud hole. The native habitat of trillions and trillions of rats and land crabs were equaled in number by the mosquitoes. We set up thousands of pyramid tents in seemingly endless rows among the coconut trees, and then began an all-day-everyday routine of cleaning the area with make-work details. The coconut trees were lined up like a checkerboard, the same as on Guadalcanal. The whole division was there. The plantation had been unattended since the war began and the ground was covered with millions of sprouting coconuts. We piled these in enormous piles as large as houses and, then, we would move the piles another couple of times, maybe several hundred yards from one location to another. To move the coconuts, we would use our worthless ponchos as nets with a man on each corner. Marines hated the issued ponchos because they only served to allow you to be soaked gradually and we preferred to simply be rained on. We were fed the old abominable C-rations for several weeks (we were back under the Navy command) until the mess tent was set up, and then the lousy corned beef, spam, beans, powdered eggs, and dehydrated potatoes returned.

On Pavuvu, there was no place to go, nothing to buy, no other units like Navy or Army to steal from, no radio, no music, no anything, just nothing to do. The high command dreamed up a task of carrying coral in our helmets, so we would trudge several blocks to a crushed coral pit all day, back and forth, and spread the white coral on our company streets and inside of our tents. We felt like Chinese coolies. A rest camp on the equator!

Clark and I went back on battalion KP when the galley tent was set up. This proved a lucky assignment as we were exempt from all the daily training and maneuvers we had endured thousands of times. My job was to tend the mess kit, washing cans for the two meals a day. There were three large galvanized steel cans in a row, on racks so a fire could be built under them to heat the water. I had to empty the old water and use fresh water for each meal. The first can had to contain chipped-up GI soap in the water and the other two were rinse water. The soap can had several small mops that hung over the edge of the can. I became an expert on getting the most heat out of the fires and gradually reduced the closest coconut piles for firewood. It was my delight to get the fires too hot and the water boiling, so it was hazardous to approach the GI cans at chow time. I couldn't be reprimanded for doing too good a job! I had an axe to chop the coconuts open and get the liquid out, and would burn only the dry coconut husks. I became an expert at this.

My series of cans for washing mess kits was set up right outside the tent of our new regimental commanding officer Colonel Lewis B. Puller. Even at that time, he was a living legend in the Marine Corps. He liked enlisted men and I enjoyed hours of conversations with him in the afternoon. He would come out of his tent before evening chow, and talk to anyone. He was a Civil War buff also and we enjoyed discussing the subject. He wanted to know what state I was from, how many were in my family, if I intended to stay in the Marine Corps, etc. When I told him I wanted to go to medical school, I remember he said that wouldn't be easy, but there was no reason why I couldn't make it if that was what I really wanted. At that time, the GI Bill had not been brought into existence. I recall how short he was, maybe five-six or seven, and that he kept a little stubby pipe going between his teeth. The thing about him that impressed me most was how genuinely friendly he was. When he asked why I was on KP, I told him and he just chuckled. Even today, when I see his picture, I am happy to know and say to myself, "I knew that man personally and liked him and he seemed to like me." There was no false air of importance about him. What a great American! Long may the legend of Chesty Puller remain in the hearts of the nation! When I was attending Spring Hill College after the war, I was approached by some local Marines to let them place my name on the roll of a local Marine reserve unit they were trying to initiate. They needed a certain minimum number of names to activate the reserve unit. I told them to forget it, but, then, they showed me in writing that I could be released at any time by simply asking for a discharge, so I relented. When I was accepted into medical school, I submitted a letter as instructed to the Commanding Officer of the Eighth Marine Corps District, New Orleans, Louisiana. Shortly thereafter, I received my second discharge from the Marine Corps dated April 6, 1948, signed by the commanding officer of the Eighth District, L. B. Puller, Colonel, U.S. Marine Corps. I like to imagine he remembered me. I bet there are very few of us with a Marine Corps discharge signed by him and I have it neatly framed and hanging in my living room.

Now, back to Pavuvu. Dear Reader, if you have read this far, you must be interested, so let me urge you to read my best friend Dr. Eugene B. Sledge's masterful book on WWII titled *With the Old Breed*. Just to whet your appetite, I am going to quote a full page from his book from the part concerning Pavuvu, because it tells what I would like to tell you, but I lack the writing skill.

This is from chapter two:

The most loathsome vermin on Pavuvu were the land crabs. Their blue-black bodies were about the size of the palm of a man's hand and bristles and spines covered their legs. These ugly creatures hid by day and roamed at night. Before putting on his boondockers each morning, every man in the 1st Marine Division shook his shoes to roust the land crabs. Many mornings I had one in each shoe and sometimes two. Periodically, we reached the point of rage over these filthy things and chased them out from under boxes, sea bags, and cots. We killed them with sticks, bayonets, and entrenching tools. After the action was over, we had to shovel them up and bury them or a nauseating stench developed rapidly in the hot, humid air.

Each battalion had its own galley, but chow on Pavuvu consisted mainly of heated C-rations; dehydrated eggs, dehydrated potatoes, and that detestable canned meat called Spam. The synthetic lemonade, so-called battery acid that remained after chow was poured on the concrete slab of the galley to clean and bleach it. It did a nice job. As if hot C-rations didn't get tedious week in and week out, we experienced a period of about four days when we were served oatmeal morning, noon, and night. Scuttlebutt was that the ship carrying our supplies had been sunk. Whatever the cause, our daily relief from monotonous chow was tidbits in packages from home. The bread made by our bakers was so heavy that when you held a slice by one side, the rest of the slice broke away from its own weight. The flour was so massively infested with weevils that each slice of bread had more of the little beetles than there are seeds in a slice of rye bread. We became so inured to this sort of thing, however, that we ate the bread anyway; the wits said "It's a good deal. Them beetles give you more meat in your diet."

We had no bathing facilities at first. Shaving each morning with a helmet full of water was simple enough, but a bath was another matter. Each afternoon when the inevitable tropical downpour commenced, we stripped and dashed into the company street, soap in hand. The trick was to lather, scrub, and rinse before the rain stopped. The weather was so capricious that the duration of a shower was impossible to estimate. Each downpour ended as abruptly as it had begun and never failed to leave at least one or more fully lathered, cursing Marines with no rinse water.

Morning sick call was another bizarre sight during the early days on Pavuvu. The Gloucester veterans were in poor physical condition after the wettest campaign in World War II, during which men endured soakings for weeks on end. When I first joined the company, I was appalled at their condition; most were thin, some emaciated, with jungle rot in their armpits and on their ankles and wrists. At sick call they paired off with a bottle of Gentian Violet and cotton swabs, stood naked in the grove, and painted each other's sores. So many of them needed attention that they had to treat each other under a doctor's supervision. Some had to cut their boondockers into sandals, because their feet were so infected with rot they could hardly walk. Needless to say, Pavuvu's hot, humid climate prolonged the healing process.

"I think the Marine Corps has forgotten where Pavuvu is," one man said.
"I think God has forgotten where Pavuvu is," came a reply.
"God couldn't forget because he made everything."
"Then I bet he wishes he could forget he made Pavuvu."

This is the end of my quote of Eugene's writing. I believe our reaction to Pavuvu was so severe because we had anticipated something much better as a reward for the Gloucester campaign.

One thing that I must emphasize and not forget is to mention the millions of large rats that inhabited Pavuvu. At night, especially when there was moonlight, they would scurry up and down the tent ropes, silhouetted against the light and as many as a half-dozen in view at one time. Strangely, they didn't seem to bother us and we didn't have any means of getting rid of them, so we mostly ignored, and simply tolerated them, even naming them. We also experienced violent earthquakes on the island. They would slosh water out of buckets that were half-full, and awaken anybody asleep.

About a month before I left Pavuvu, we were informed that some of us remaining old-timers would get to return to the states on a rotation plan. As I recall, about half of us originals would get to leave, and half must remain. For the mortar platoon, about thirty small pieces of paper were placed into a helmet, half were blank and half had numbers on them. The helmet was held high in the air and we formed a line in alphabetical order to pass by so each could draw out a piece of paper. The rules were, if we pulled out two pieces of paper, we forfeited our turn and chance to draw; so everyone felt very carefully before he withdrew a piece of paper. W.O. drew a number, I drew a number, Deacon drew a blank, Luke drew a blank, Ransom drew a blank. Benny must have drawn a number in the officers' category because his name was posted to return to the states also. Then the Marines with numbers were divided into two groups alphabetically. The first half would depart on the first ship and the second half would depart on the second ship. My old high school pal, Eugene B. Sledge, came in on the first ship as a replacement, unknown to me, and my old pal W.O. Brown, being in the first half of the alphabet, departed on the ship that brought Eugene in. They did not see each other.

The next day after W.O. left, I was sitting on my cot when I noticed someone coming down the company street looking in each tent. I recognized Ugin (his nickname) about three tents away and ran out into the company street, screaming "Ugin" as loudly as I could. He ran and I ran; we hugged each other and pounded on each other, and rolled around wrestling on the ground, shouting and screaming. A large crowd gathered, thinking we were fighting, and I introduced him around and then we went back to pounding on each other. For the two weeks until I departed, we would get together every afternoon and night and talk until the wee hours. By this time, we old-timers had become experts at making and hiding jungle juice and did our best to have a party whenever a new batch was ready. The difficult part was getting the basic ingredients of canned fruit. Ugin and I particularly enjoyed the movies, now maybe three times a week, and would go together and roll in laughter at the obscene remarks that were shouted by the comedians as they tried to outperform the script during every love scene. The theater was open-air with coconut logs for seats. He would arrive early enough from his camp with the Fifth Marines to help me with my galley chores after evening chow. Seldom would the film projector go more than ten minutes without a breakdown and delay, causing a hilarious chorus of groans and curses.

Probably about a week before I left Pavuvu, it was announced that Bob Hope would arrive and put on his show the next day. We had never had anything like this in my whole two years overseas. Naturally, I caught division guard duty at the very hours of the show and was one of the very few Marines who could not be there. I was feeling sorry for myself and walking my lonely post at the division water point, the only person there, when a truck passed by with some men standing in the back. A big guy with a huge mustache bellowed at me and waved, not fifteen yards away. Startled, I waved back rather feebly; then the truck was gone. Then, it dawned on me: that had been Jerry Colonna with the Bob Hope show and that he had given me one of his famous yells just for myself. He never knew what that did for my morale. I was all alone, so I just sat down and cried a little bit. It seemed one of my countrymen did care about me in that isolated, forlorn place after all.

The story goes around that when the final Marine rear echelon departed from Pavuvu, millions and millions of rats and land crabs came down to the dock and made obscene ges-

205

tures to let it be known that Pavuvu was the only Pacific island
the First Marine Division could not conquer.

Those of us being rotated never felt we were ever really
going to leave Pavuvu, that we were only going to awaken
from a dream, until we boarded ship and pulled away.

19

As the bus was coming into Mobile, I thought I would wake up and find myself on Pavuvu.

═══════════════

As our ship pulled away from Pavuvu, we simply could not believe we were alive and experiencing this departure. Another old-timer, Dave Madison, from Atmore, Alabama, a member of H Company and close friend, was with me. Dave was a corporal in one of the machine gun platoons and Dave and I immediately became closer cobbers for the trip. Every Marine liked to have a cobber to be with and talk to. *Cobber* is the

Australian equivalent of "buddy." Sometimes, names would almost be forgotten as cobber served as a substitute. We had no duties assigned on this large new ship with twin screws and we traveled east, gloriously east alone and at a very fast clip. We came into the harbor at San Diego about ten in the morning; there was a Marine band there on the dock playing "Semper Fidelis," "Stars and Stripes Forever," and then they blared out with "Dixie," and all of us Southerners lost our cool and cried. We had not heard any music since leaving Melbourne except the one comic show on Goodenough. As we filed down the gangplank with our old worn packs and gear, but no weapons as they had remained overseas on Pavuvu, many got down on their knees and kissed the dock.

We were taken to the Marine depot at San Diego in trucks and placed in a tent city close to the main buildings. We were given an advance of pay, maybe twenty dollars. We were not allowed to leave the base, but had access to the PX (Post Exchange) and could buy anything we wanted. We turned in our old tired equipment and were issued new sea bags and clothing. Our stay there lasted about two weeks as we were processed for new assignments, took tests, a cursory medical exam, and filled out papers. I wrote my family that I was back in the U.S.A. and would be home as soon as we were processed. It was very difficult in 1944 to make a long-distance phone call. Sometimes doing so required an hour just to make connections, if you could get to a phone. There would be twenty-five or more

Marines in line for the few phones available, and the line would not move, so I gave up after a couple of attempts and just wrote a letter. One of my clearest memories was our first meal in the huge chow hall. Food was actually offered cafeteria-style, and we lean, atabrine yellow, old-timers were a curiosity to the thousands of Marines who were there on the base. Dave Madison and I started through the chow line with our trays and first came to the lettuce. We asked if there was any limit on the lettuce and, when told there was not, we loaded our trays with nothing but lettuce. The lettuce was cut into one-fourth head wedges, and we went back again and again for more. A crowd of curious mess men gathered around us and watched us eat lettuce, and eat lettuce, and eat lettuce. We hadn't had any lettuce for over two years; Australians didn't eat lettuce. We each ate about twelve wedges of it.

Another clear memory is our first freshwater shower there and how Dave and I lathered and rinsed repeatedly for at least an hour until we were squeaky clean. There had been no freshwater showers on the troop ship.

Finally, we left San Diego on a troop train with Benny in charge of us on the train, headed for the East Coast. We were deliriously happy as the train shrieked eastward and I remember standing in a vestibule between cars for hours as we crossed Louisiana, drinking in the scenery of the Southland and the smell and sight of the longleaf pines. Benny knew the train route, and it was through New Orleans, then north to Meridian, and east to Birmingham toward New York. Dave and I opted to depart in Meridian, climbed off with our sea bags, and waved goodbye to the guys as they pulled out.

We checked schedules; the fastest way to Mobile was by bus, so Dave and I walked to the bus station carrying our sea bags and used our government chit for tickets to Mobile, checked our sea bags, and walked around Meridian for several hours to kill time. As the bus was coming into Mobile, I thought I would wake up and find myself on Pavuvu. Dave said he had the same sensation. We unloaded in the Mobile bus station; I couldn't remember my own phone number and had to look it up in the tattered phone book. This was August 1944. Almost immediately, Dave caught a bus to Fairhope where a sister was living. I carried my sea bag out to the curb in front of the bus station on Government Street and waited for the arrival of my family, wondering if I could keep my cool. They arrived in a few minutes, and we all went through a rather wild tearful time of greeting and hugging. I felt as if I had been gone from Mobile for at least twenty years and found the strangely crowded city unlike anything I had imagined.

My family treated me as if I had returned from the grave and we stayed up and talked until almost dawn. Then, I went to bed in my old bed and could not close my eyes because of the excitement. I had a whole month of furlough before I had to report to my new base.

Ugin had written to his family telling them I was on the

way home from Pavuvu; Mrs. Sledge had called before I arrived home to offer me one of their cars to drive while I was home. It was a little Ford coupe that Dr. Sledge used for bird hunting and smelled like a dog pound. The next day after I had arrived, Mother drove me out to the Sledge home, known as "The Georgia Cottage," and I picked up the car. It was full of gas and had good tires. I was so cocky; I just drove it downtown to the courthouse, took a driver's test, told the policeman a bunch of war stories, and drove away with a driver's license.

Good luck prevailed and two of my closest friends happened to get leave from the Army while I was home for the month of August, each for about a week. Chibby Smith came first and then George Edgar. Needless to say, I enjoyed a wild good time. On one day, I called Dave Madison, went over to Fairhope, and we spent the entire day drinking beer at the Gulf. We used a nail keg full of ice for a cooler. I can't remember where Dave was being sent, but it was not where I was going. On the last day of my leave, George and I were walking through the Merchant's Bank when George stopped to speak to a girl he knew in his class at Murphy High School, which was the class of 1942. This was now 1944. She was working as a bank teller. I nearly collapsed right on the floor. She was the same girl I had always thought was the prettiest girl in Murphy. When I was at Murphy, I worked in the school cafeteria and punched the cash register for the girl's chow line. Her name was Mary Houston. I was an expert girl-watcher and I had drooled over her for two years in high school, but knew there was no chance such a pretty girl would remain single long enough for me to go to college and be in a position to get married. There she stood, still unmarried, due to the war, as most of the boys were in the military. She was even prettier than I had remembered. My leave was up and I had to leave Mobile the next day. I felt like the world's greatest dunce; I could have been getting to know the world's prettiest girl for a whole month.

My new base was Boca Chica Naval Air Station, Boca Chica, Florida. The train trip to Miami would have required much more time than the bus, so I opted to go by bus. I left Mobile, standing in the aisle; sometimes I could sit on a suitcase, but did not get a seat until the bus reached Miami. Can you imagine that trip? It took over twenty-four hours to reach Miami. In the Miami bus station, I met some more recently returned First Division Marines, also bound for Boca Chica.

We found Boca Chica was really Key West because it was only about seven miles north. It was a huge U.S. Naval air training station for pilots who had completed their basic Pensacola training. The U.S. No.1 highway to Key West divided the naval base, which was on both sides of the highway since Boca Chica Key wasn't very wide. The bus stopped at the main gate and dumped us and our sea bags. We soon found nearly the entire Marine unit had just been replaced with returned First Division Marines. We were furious and miserable. We found ourselves happy to be in the states, but angered to be back in the tropics again and in such an isolated place. Miami was too far, except with a weekend pass, and there were no girls in Key West, so, once again, there was nothing to do except one's duty. The town of Key West was actually one gigantic bar composed of one tiny bar next to another tiny bar, with several large bars that hosted dancing strip-tease shows. I found three or four new cobbers, Murdock from Tennessee, Freelon Smith from Birmingham, and Bill Newell from Miami. We went into Key West about three times and then decided there was no purpose in that; we would just sit in the PX on the base at Boca Chica and drink bottled beer made in Philadelphia by Schmidt's Brewery (not Schlitz). It was fifteen cents a bottle and the only brand available. I recall on one of my trips into Key West, I had too much to drink in that heat and passed out from too much booze. I recall being kicked awake and looking up from the floor in a strip-tease joint into the faces of two swabbie SPs, then quickly surrounded by my cobbers who told the SPs to shove off, that they would take me back to the base, which they did. For some reason, I can clearly recall a girl bumping and grinding right by my right elbow to the tune of the "Hawaiian War Chant." She was covered with sweat and even her hair was wringing wet. My thought was, up close she isn't very attractive and then I slid to the floor. Deacon would have given me several of his long lectures.

There was a twenty-foot-high wooden ramp with stairs

maybe six feet wide that crossed the highway from one side of the base to the other; any military pedestrian was required to climb the ramp and walk over it to go from one side of the base to the other. The sailors had cut holes in the chain link fences and would dash across the highway to keep from climbing the stupid ramp. The new First "Divvy" Marines put a stop to that by shooting at the sailors, not intending to hit them, but just to get their attention. There was nothing to hit for miles north and south on the highway and almost no traffic. We were soon known as mean and bad Pacific veterans and we had to uphold the reputation.

I recall one day when I was on the main gate, a Navy station wagon complete with enlisted driver and four Navy captains (four-stripers) drove up to the gate. One captain had no I.D. card, yet they started to drive on through. I placed my hand on my revolver and told them to stop, made them all get out and go into the guard house for clearance. This was all done with firm politeness and snappy salutes. That was the only post I ever stood in the Marine Corps where we were armed with a revolver. I suppose this released .45 automatics for overseas. We had 03 Springfields for the other guard posts. We had the authority to make anybody driving off the base stop, get out, and open the trunk of his vehicle for inspection, which we would do regularly just to be hateful, keep up our reputation, and break the boring monotony.

One of our posts was guard on a gasoline dump with underground storage tanks, way down the runway, about a mile from the tower, and just on the edge of the government property. It had a little screened shack about the size of six telephone booths with a table in it and nobody had any reason to be there except Navy gasoline trucks. When assigned this post, we could depend on four hours of nothing but nothing. Marines with severe hangovers or the flu or any illness could sit in the little shack and see the guard jeep coming down the runway for five minutes before it arrived. In the midnight-to-four watches on that post, I would sometimes sing as loudly, and as badly, as I could; I would even scream to see if I could get anybody's attention and never did.

We were housed in a long wooden, one-story barracks, with double-decked bunks, foot lockers, and wall lockers. Routine Saturday morning inspections were a farce. Foot lockers were never opened for inspection and we kept a complete extra set of inspection clothing in our foot lockers that we hauled out and placed in the wall lockers neatly and precisely with stenciled names showing; then, after inspection, everything in the lockers was reversed. We could get ready for inspection in about five minutes. Discipline was not severe and we had some excellent NCOs.

In this nearly tropical heat, it was the custom to walk the short distance over to the showers and head which were in separate buildings wearing exactly nothing, sometimes a towel. Then, we came back wearing nothing and maybe stood by the ironing board at the end of the barracks to iron our khaki shirts and pants wearing the same nothing. The iron almost never cooled off and was the collective property of the barracks. When an officer entered the building, it was necessary for all hands to rise and stand at attention, and, frequently, a false alarm would be sounded by some comedian to try to embarrass whoever was naked and ironing at the moment. Into this scenario, one day, an admiral and other high-ranking naval inspection officers did enter unannounced and unexpected. The loud call "ATTENTION" was given and a naked ironer, thinking it was a comedian and a false alarm, did not even turn around and answered with some loud foul invective to knock off that foolishness. He finally looked around after some repeated calls and faced the admiral and officers in his absolutely no-clothes situation. The admiral and officers had the good manners to walk on through the barracks, while we dissolved in a fit of laughter at the naked, embarrassed ironer.

One of our regular daily duties was to pull colors (raise and lower the flag), and this was supposed to be done at precisely the moment of sunrise and sunset, with as much military snap and sharpness (no nonsense) as possible. We would march in step, heads up, shoulders back, and stand at rigid attention at the base of the flagstaff, with the sergeant pretending to look at his watch, waiting for the precise moment to pull colors. We were actually stalling and waiting for as high-ranking an officer as possible to drive by, preferably, at least a captain. When the bugler would begin to blow colors, all cars had to stop and the occupants climb out, stand at attention, and salute facing the flag. We enjoyed this and no one objected to "pulling colors."

As I recall, we had only one Marine officer at Boca Chica, a major. He had some physical infirmity and walked with a slight limp. The scuttlebutt was that he could not pass the physical for overseas duty and resented us all being returned from overseas. We almost never saw him. We had an excellent top sergeant, I wish I could remember his name, but I cannot. I do remember it was Irish and started with "Mc." Reading the bulletin board one day, I found a notice about a program called V12, which was, in essence, an officers' training program. Being an officer was not my goal, but I was extremely anxious to start getting some college credits. I went in to see the top sergeant; he had me sit down and we went over the papers together. He was enthusiastic and said I had the highest score that he had ever seen on the general aptitude test we had taken in San Diego, and that I certainly was eligible to apply. He then told me the application required an officer's recommendation and signature; he knew the major would never sign it, but he had an idea: for me to be patient, trust him, and wait. There was an annual inspection at the end of the year by a high-ranking officer from Washington, D.C., and this was nearly upon us. The Saturday of the inspection soon arrived and the inspecting officer was a full colonel named Hill wearing a First Marine Division patch on his shoulder and the same ribbons we all wore. He was from the staff of the Marine Commandant General Vandergrift and one of us. After the inspection, we were all standing at attention and being commended with a pep talk by Colonel Hill when he announced he would be in the office for an hour; if anybody wanted to talk to him about anything, to feel free to do so. As he said this, the top sergeant looked right at me and nodded his head ever so slightly.

When dismissed, I put away my gear, rushed over to the office, asked permission to speak to the colonel, and stated my case. The top sergeant told the colonel that I qualified; he had my papers ready and they only needed an officer's signature. The colonel looked them over, signed them and put them in his briefcase, turned to me and told me to pack my sea bag, that the papers would be on the commandant's desk Monday morning and I should be getting transfer papers by Wednesday. He said this was the very thing the commandant had told him to be on the lookout for. He then asked me if I had ever met the commandant and I told him about the soap episode in the Lunga River. He laughed long and loudly and said, "He will remember it exactly." I saluted and floated out of the office. I wanted to hug the top sergeant.

On Wednesday morning, I was summoned to the office and the top sergeant said, "Here are your papers. You catch the bus at the main gate in one hour." My cobbers carried my sea bag out to the main gate, and bid me goodbye, and away I went from that awful place, deliriously happy once again. The bus had plenty of room and I sat in the third seat back from the front on the starboard side and talked to the guys through the open window before we pulled out for Miami. It seemed the pattern in the service was to constantly alternate between mountaintops of joy and deep valleys of misery.

20

Then, out of the door came Mary Victoria
Houston, dressed in a navy blue, polka-dot
dress and high heels with her brown curly hair
bouncing. I actually became dizzy . . .

====

Arriving in the Miami bus station, I found the train station was only a short distance away, maybe two blocks, so I just shouldered my sea bag and walked to it. Taxi cabs were almost nonexistent. A serviceman carrying all of his gear was not an unusual sight during the war. Using my government chit, I purchased a train ticket to Wilmington, North Carolina, as my orders read, to report to a certain numbered building at Camp Lejeune by a certain time on a given date (two days as I recall, not enough time to go by Mobile). My train ride was uneventful, except it required that I sit up all night in a day coach (no Pullman sleeper), then I took the bus from Wilmington to Camp Lejeune. I alighted with sea bag at the main gate, wearing greens (it was January), and showed my orders to the gate sergeant. He stopped a jeep and I was given a ride with my sea bag to the specified building, which was one of a number of large new brick barracks. There was almost nothing that looked familiar from the old New River base of two years ago.

Walking inside carrying my sea bag, I reported to a sergeant at a desk in the foyer and turned in my papers. He checked his list of names, found mine, and told me to go into the barracks and choose any empty bunk of the standard doubled-decked. I did so and began to meet the other Marines who were already there; when someone asked me what state I was from, I answered Alabama in a loud voice; and a huge guy added, "What city?" When I answered, "Mobile," he said, "Me, too." Thus began my close friendship with Marion "Bunk" Sims. I moved my gear next to Bunk's and I knew I had found my new cobber. He was as big as Tex. Bunk had been returned from the Pacific for the V12 program, and was a veteran of the Saipan and Tinian campaigns. We were told the Marine Corps was experimenting with the idea of putting combat veterans into the V12 program because so many V12 students had been intentionally flunking out of the program so they could get into a combat unit. Our group at Camp Lejeune numbered about two hundred.

It was understood that your rank was reduced to private when you were accepted in V12, and this meant a severe reduction in pay and position for some of the applicants who might have been staff sergeants. Bunk had been a corporal. To further test us applicants, we were put through a severe three weeks of boot camp–style discipline, that made some of the guys decide the program was not for them. They could return to their former stations at their previous ranks. Actually, the discipline for those three weeks was every bit as bad as Parris Island's, and maybe even worse. I was young and strong and took it gladly to get into the program, as did Bunk. We had had enough of the mud, troop ships, and C-rations. It was also understood that V12 was for single men only; if you got married, you were automatically expelled from the program and remained a private. We were to remain privates in the program until commissioned as second lieutenants. The indoctrination period ended and Bunk and I and maybe twenty more of the two hundred were assigned to the Marine V12 unit at the University of North Carolina at Chapel Hill. We were given orders to report there in about ten days and, thus, had ten days' furlough. We were on the mountaintop again. We shipped our sea bags to Chapel Hill, bought small handbags to carry a few changes of clothing, and started hitchhiking to Mobile. Never could I have wanted a better friend than Bunk.

It was February 1945 when Bunk and I arrived in Mobile for more than a week of furlough. Dr. and Mrs. Sledge offered the little Ford again, so I headed for the Merchants Bank to see if that gorgeous teller was still there and not married. She was there with no ring on her finger, so I filled out a counter check to withdraw fifteen dollars from my account and approached her window. This was all a pretense to have a reason to stand there and talk to her. I introduced myself and told her I had met her the previous August there in the bank with George Edgar. She cooed, "Oh, yes, I remember." After some chitchat, she agreed to let me drive her home after work at 3:30, but added I would have to meet her outside as the inside would be closed to the public. I was prompt; in fact, about ten minutes early, and spent the time talking to the old bank guard in his fancy green uniform with gold epaulets and fourrageres standing outside the door entrance, telling him war stories—some of which might have been true.

Then, out of the door came Mary Victoria Houston, dressed in a navy blue, polka-dot dress and high heels with her brown curly hair bouncing. I actually became dizzy; I had it bad! I took her hand to help her across St. Joseph Street, as though she was helpless and could not walk unassisted, and then released it. We walked along St. Francis Street, with me properly on the outside. I noticed in the plate glass windows, that acted as mirrors, that every male would turn and look back at her. You could see in the faces of all the soldiers and sailors going by that they could not comprehend a lowly private with all those overseas ribbons escorting Miss America.

I explained to Mary that the car smelled like a dog pound, but she just cooed that she didn't mind at all, that she loved dogs. As we reached Conception Street, it dawned on me that I didn't have a clue as to where I had parked the car. My mind was blank and would not function. I stammered that I had been downtown all day and had moved the car several times (a total lie) and wasn't sure where it was. She cooed not to worry, that she knew where I would park; we went to the parking lot by the old jail and there the car was. When I asked her how she knew, she replied that her family always parked there when they came to town. Was that logical?

We drove up Old Shell Road, turned on Dogwood Lane, and parked in her driveway on Stein Street. Her father was out in the front yard and I met him, putting on my best manners and giving him a firm handshake. He was testing an electric lawn mower that he had assembled from old parts, including an electric fan motor, making a contraption that may have been a new invention. It really interested me as he explained it. Then, I met Mrs. Houston, trying not to use any foul language and reviewing my father's ancient instructions in good manners, such as, "When a lady is standing, you stand; when a lady sits, you may sit." I seemed to pass their inspection and received permission to return that night and take Mary to a movie. Never has any young man tried to be more proper and correct. It was a well-known problem among servicemen during the war that when a person went home on furlough, he might inadvertently lapse into an unintentional release of foul language, and this concern was always in the forefront of my thinking. It caused me to speak slowly and carefully. Mary and I seemed to like and dislike the same things. I was a hopeless basket case of adoration for her. She revealed that she was the youngest in her family, with six older brothers, four of them in the Navy and three of them officers. I knew they would not care for their beautiful little sister to be dating a common Marine private. I, therefore, tried to pretend to have good sense. Everything lacking in my personality hers seemed to fulfill. Where I tended to be naturally a little shy, she was outgoing and could enter a room full of men and charm them all in minutes. Where I tended to procrastinate, she would finish anything that needed to be done, right away. We had a date every night that I was in Mobile. If ever there were two people perfectly matched for each other, it was we two. My furlough quickly passed and Bunk and I hitchhiked to Chapel Hill. Mary and I exchanged letters twice a week.

Chapel Hill was heaven on earth to a Marine private. We had one officer, a captain and maybe four sergeants who were in the regular Marine Corps. Discipline was relaxed. Our unit numbered about two hundred. We were housed in an ancient building known as Old East, with the school symbol, an old well, right outside. After a few months, we were moved into a large three-story brick dormitory called Grimes Hall. In Grimes, we had six to a room with three double-decked bunks, three dressers with drawers for our clothes, and two closets to hang up our uniforms. There were large tables for study with nice desk lamps. We had laundry service and ate in a large Navy mess hall. The Navy had a large unit of V12 for what was called pre-flight training, with the ultimate end becoming Navy pilots. Classes were six days a week all day and I really had to keep my nose in the books. I performed well and made good grades. Bunk and another roommate were on the football team. We only had inspections on Saturday mornings and they consisted only of having a clean, neat room. We had close order drill one afternoon each week for only two hours and without any weapons. No weapons were issued. Semesters were super-accelerated, so we started a new semester about every two months. We would get a week off between semesters and, then, Bunk and I would go to Mobile.

There was a Marine there from New Orleans named Begnaud whose nickname, naturally, was Frenchy. Frenchy had an old Chevrolet convertible with a non-functional top of rags that was kept folded back. If it rained, the passengers got wet.

He kept it covered at Chapel Hill with a tarp and parked on a side street. We would go with Frenchy to make the trip to Mobile, sharing expenses. Four of us would make the trip, dropping one boy off in Atlanta. The old car was painted blue and we called it "The Blue Goose." Frenchy's brother had a used car lot in New Orleans, and if Frenchy could get to New Orleans, his brother could get used car parts. None were available in Chapel Hill at any price. These trips in the Blue Goose were memorable and wild. We were all able to get gas ration coupons by applying as though we had automobiles. On one trip, we left Chapel Hill in the Blue Goose with a non-functioning generator. There was almost no traffic on the nation's highways and, if we kept the lights off, the battery would provide ignition for hundreds of miles; then, we could get a quick recharge on the battery. We would tailgate a truck, with the truck driver's knowledge, all night. As we came through Mobile on Highway 90 (Government Street), I would jump out at Catherine Street and the Blue Goose would roll on with Bunk jumping out at the Loop. The Blue Goose had four spare tires, and all eight tires needed to be thrown away. Most of the tires were worn through the rubber, exposing the yellow fabric inside. Our top speed was fifty miles per hour. On one trip, we left Chapel Hill in the late afternoon with snow on the ground, a full moon, and no generator for lights. There was almost no traffic, so we could fly down the black highway with snow on both sides with perfect visibility. It was so cold, our feet became numb even though we had on our green wool uniforms and overcoats and were covered with our blankets. We stopped and got doubled grocery bags to stick our feet in, which worked great. This was before the days of plastic bags.

On another trip, the brakes went out due to a leak in the brake hydraulic system. We could get plenty of brake fluid, so we would stop and fill the master cylinder before entering a town. We then had brakes, of a sort, for about ten or fifteen minutes with wild vigorous pumping of the brake pedal. I recall one event, probably in Atlanta, the street was redbrick and we were in a steep downhill situation with the Blue Goose picking up speed every second. Frenchy managed to get the Goose into second gear, but we continued to accelerate at an alarming pace. We could see a cross street coming up about two blocks away with heavy traffic and streetcars. Frenchy was pumping and pumping the brake pedal and screaming, "No brakes!" We all got on the running boards of the Goose, ready to jump. Frenchy had the driver's door open standing on the running board in front of me, and steering with one hand as we rocketed downhill. I know we were doing fifty or more and the Goose was complaining in a wild, screaming wail about being in second gear. Miraculously, like the Red Sea for Moses, the traffic had a three-second lull and parted as we went through the intersection, screaming in terror and ready to jump. I am certain the Lord opened that traffic for us. Frenchy managed to curb the Goose to a halt when the road leveled off and we all got out and laid on the ground until our hearts stopped pounding. Then we refilled the brake cylinder and went on.

We each had a number for changing a tire; I was number three. Number one was the jack man, number two the lug man, number three got the spare ready and stored the flat away. Frenchy was number four and barked orders in a loud voice like a drill sergeant. Our record time for a change was one minute, fifteen seconds, timed by Frenchy, always nonsense. Trips back to Chapel Hill were usually not too hectic because the Goose would have had all bad parts replaced with other second-hand parts that would, at least, function for a while. I recall we stopped to get gas in a small town and Bunk asked the teenage boy pumping gas, "Where is the HEAD, fellow?" The boy left, and brought back a man, and said, "Here is the head fellow." They could not understand our laughter.

While in Mobile on one of these short furloughs, I met Bunk's parents. They proved to be young at heart and decided they wanted to come to see us in North Carolina. They offered Mary a chance to accompany them. Mary said, "yes," and her parents gave their consent. She spent all of her savings to make the trip. Bunk's girlfriend also made the trip. They came by train and we met them in Greensboro, North Carolina, but found there was no way time would permit a bus trip to Chapel Hill. We spent a well-chaperoned weekend in Greensboro, but I knew Mary was going to be my choice for a lifetime.

I recall on VJ Day (victory over Japan and the end of WWII), almost the entire student body built a gigantic bonfire in the middle of the main street in Chapel Hill. It set the asphalt pavement on fire and burned up the traffic light hanging in the middle of the intersection. The little Chapel Hill fire truck came and hooked to a fire hydrant and pumped water on the whole mess. The Chapel Hill police department arrived to restore order and the guys good-naturedly picked them up and carried them to their car and waved them goodbye. Our semester ended at Christmas in 1945, and we came to Mobile in the Blue Goose for my first Christmas at home since 1941. I spent every penny I had to buy Mary a watch; she pouted and said she wanted a ring. My four-year enlistment expired on December 31, 1945. Bunk and I returned to Chapel Hill in the Blue Goose, picked up our gear, took the bus to Camp Lejeune, and were discharged. The V12 program was disbanded and I had two full years of college credits to take into civilian life, plus four years of G.I. Bill time to continue my education. I felt the Marine Corps had really been good to me.

I had entered the Marine Corps as a seventeen-year-old private, and came out four years and six days later as a twenty-one-year-old private. Actually, I was promoted to corporal on the date of discharge. Mary and I were married on April 15, 1946, her twenty-first birthday, by two ministers with Eugene Bondurant Sledge acting as best man. Thank goodness the Japs bombed Pearl Harbor! It kept the boys away from Mary until I could grow up.

Reflections

=====

When I finished these memoirs in 1998, my wife, Mary, and I were both seventy-three years young and she was still in good health. But, in 2000, Mary cheated, and beat me to heaven. We made an agreement that we would both live to be 130, in good health, and both die the same night in each others' arms. She died with leukemia four days after our fifty-fourth wedding anniversary at the age of seventy-five. I will be okay and get over her death in about twenty-five more years. I am not concerned about the spiritual; it's just the plain simple loneliness and no one telling me constantly how wonderful I am.

I had twenty copies of the memoirs printed before her death and distributed them to my family. They were received with such astounding enthusiasm that I had to have another twenty copies printed and distributed to friends with corrections of misspelled words and place names. Then a hundred copies with a few more corrections and I began to offer them for sale. Then another hundred copies and then another hundred copies were necessary. Now, it's become a hardcover book for distribution around the world—a development I never saw coming.

Eugene Sledge's family, i.e., his charming widow, Miss Jeanne, and his sons, John and Henry, directed the interviewers for the Ken Burns documentary, *The War*, to me and my sister, Katharine. We were caught up in the Ken Burns documentary and I gave the Ken Burns team a copy of the memoirs. Katharine and I were able to provide the interviewers a large amount of accurate information and photographs they needed about the childhood and high school days of Eugene Bondurant Sledge. Eugene had hated his middle name of Bondurant, so I frequently called him Bondurant; he would retaliate by calling me by my family nickname, "Buddy," which I hated.

Then, again through the Sledge family, my sister, Katharine, and I were included in the interviews for the miniseries, *The Pacific*, in Hollywood, being produced by Tom Hanks and Steven Spielberg. I am told there will be four central characters in the movie: John Basilone, Robert Leckie, Eugene Sledge, and Sid Phillips. Robert Leckie was in my company H-2-1 in WWII and I am to be a link between characters. I am the only one of the characters still alive and have been able to give the writers detailed information when needed. This has been a delightful experience for both my sister and me in our old age.

That I am caught up in this as a celebrity is incomprehensible to me, except to see it as the work of The Almighty. That a seventeen-year-old private first-class nobody, in the rear rank of the Marine Corps, who was simply there during some wild days and nights for four years of WWII has become a celebrity is amazing to me. I recall when I was a boy I saw an article in the newspaper about the death of one of the old Confederate soldiers who had been a drummer boy at the Battle of Shiloh. Now I feel almost as if I know exactly how he must have felt with his notoriety in his old age.

If I am asked for my opinion today, I enjoy giving it, but I also explain opinions are just that. They can be right or wrong, true or false, or a mixture. Some people believe absolute truth exists; some people believe truth can be only relative. I believe we are always searching for absolute truth and it must exist. I am a scientist and a Christian and I believe truth can be absolute; in fact, absolute truth must exist or reason is ultimately futile. With relative truth, we can continually improve things as more data is learned, e.g., the improvement of the telescope or the computer. Absolute truth scientifically would require all data, and this means a knowledge of all things past, present, and future, which is omniscience; since man cannot have omniscience, only God can expound absolute truth. So, man must look to God's word for absolute truth. To me, this is profoundly simple and comforting. I believe compromising Scripture in the past and trying to make it say what it does not say has been man's greatest blunder.

Also, as a scientist I know science is the systematic study of earthly things and biological evolution is impossible. There simply is no process for it. For biological evolution to occur, information must be easily and naturally added to the DNA in the genome. What a tremendous psychological advantage it is to understand this. Darwin's concept of evolution through natural selection is the opposite of evolution. Natural selection is a well-known actual biological process, but it results from the loss of information from the genome.

I find most men want the same things, whether they be liberal or conservative or Republican or Democrat. They want peace, love, joy, hope, charity, faith, virtue, temperance, holiness, truth, and wisdom, albeit these things are only obtainable as gifts of the Spirit of God. They cannot be obtained by any other means. We never seem to learn and retain this.

In my opinion, the best troops we have ever put in the field have been the troops since WWII. In WWII, we fought the enemy and the enemies were Japan and Germany. Since WWII, we have fought the bad guys among the good guys and anyone with common sense knows this is next to impossible, especially if the good guys won't help. Ask any policeman. Politicians now run the wars. This is wrong. The military should run the wars and war should be declared by Congress so the majority of people will be in support. In my opinion, what has happened since WWII will destroy our sovereignty and existence as a Christian nation. It sends a message that we cannot win wars. I hope the American people can awaken again as they did after Pearl Harbor was attacked. It was thrilling to be a part of that group of American Jarheads who could go from outrageous comedy to deadly serious ferocity in seconds. It is strange how I have such a clear memory of so many things that happened during WWII. One thing I remember so vividly was that the media did not try to divide us.

I have been asked frequently who I think were the real heroes in war and the answer to that is so easy. They were the ones who did not come back and those who were badly wounded, physically or mentally.

Another thing that I love to talk about is the 1942 snapshots I have been pictured in as I rise to "celebrity status." No blue uniforms were issued to Marines in WWII unless you were stationed aboard ship as part of the Marine detachment. We were given a seventy-two-hour pass on Memorial Day weekend in May 1942. We had never had more than a forty-eight-hour pass. We all knew this meant we were shipping out of the U.S. very soon as our 5th and 7th regiments had already gone from camp. Blue uniforms were permissible to be worn, but only a few old-timers possessed one. A Marine in my company had one and offered it for rent for the weekend for twenty dollars. It would barely fit me and the cover was one-fourth of a size too small, but my friend W.O. Brown pitched in five bucks and I rented it to increase our odds for getting a ride when hitchhiking. W.O. and I had decided if we were unable to get rides, that when half of our seventy-two hours was gone, we would simply turn around and start back. The uniform did prove to stop cars and W.O. and I made steady progress south. The only time I ever had on a dress blue uniform was the forty-eight hours of that weekend, but now I am a celebrity in a blue uniform.

I love to remember my uncle Joe Tucker. He was born in 1907 and always was a most unusual character. He enlisted in the Navy in the 1920s and would visit us frequently when I was a boy as he was stationed sixty miles away in Pensacola for a couple of years. His entire Navy career was in the air branch; I recall he was an excellent mechanic and, in the 1930s took my father's old car engine completely apart and rebuilt it without telling my father he was going to do it. This took a couple of days and Dad was most apprehensive. I remember Uncle Joe was a mechanic on several of the huge dirigibles the Navy had in the 1930s and served on most of our early aircraft carriers. After WWII, Uncle Joe told me the best thing that had ever happened for the Navy was the Japanese attack on Pearl Harbor. Sinking all those battleships let the old admirals know that the Navy must begin to enter the air age in a big way. The Pearl Harbor attack didn't frighten Uncle Joe at all when they missed getting our carriers. It just made him angry as hell. He was commissioned and put on the new carrier *York-town* and, when the war ended, was a full commander. What a debt the nation owes to all of those Uncle Joe Navy chiefs who were there in the Navy to step forward after the Pearl Harbor attack and, of course, all the old NCOs in the Marine Corps and Army.

In my opinion, there is or was a great deal more humor among American troops, especially Marines, than historians realize. I think people should know this. My platoon, I believe, was composed of about 50 percent clowns and each clown seemed to compete for first place. I know and appreciate the fact that this was a means of ignoring and sweeping tension under the rug, but it was there and I wish movies and documentaries could put more of it in. I can still see PFC Ransom running for our squad hole on Guadalcanal when the bombs or shells started to rain in, screaming "Everybody stay calm and don't lose your head or go to pieces!" Also, we Marines lived in a world of sarcasm and bad language. Nothing complimentary or encouraging was ever heard. I was repeatedly told I was so stupid I couldn't pour urine out of a boot with directions on the heel. If someone said something civil to you, it was almost a sign they didn't like you. I recall returning to my unit from the hospital in Melbourne after hepatitis and greeted, "Damn Phillips, is that you? You look terrible! What a revolting development this is! We were wishing you would

die and we wouldn't have to look at your ugly face anymore!"
I knew I was home again with my cobbers.

There was almost something religious or spiritual permeating WWII. *Webster's Dictionary* defines a religion as a system of belief based upon faith. All men (a generic term for men and women) are very religious creatures by *Webster's* definition. Atheism is, in fact, a religion because faith in the idea that the God idea is only a lot of hooey is a very strong faith. It takes more faith to be an atheist than to believe in God, so the unbeliever is more religious than the believer. I wish the Supreme Court could understand it. We can make golf or football or fishing a religion.

In a splendid book by Tom Brokaw, *The Greatest Generation*, Brokaw speaks of my generation, yet he may not have the title correct. We were undoubtedly a great generation, but I believe the greatest generation of Americans is yet to come and will be the generation that turns our nation back to God.

Dr. Sid Phillips was born September 2, 1924, and enlisted in the United States Marine Corps the day after Pearl Harbor, because the Marines promised to put him "eyeball-to-eyeball" with the Japanese. Passing beneath the Golden Gate Bridge, he departed his land a nervous seventeen-year-old. Two years later, when he kissed the docks in San Diego, he had come home a hero. Together, Sid and his brothers in the legendary 1st Marine Division won the first epic victory of the war, saved Australia, and stopped the Japanese juggernaut in the Pacific. Today, Sid enjoys his golden years surrounded by his family. He and his sister, Katharine, have become internationally known after their notable roles in Ken Burns's documentary *The War*, and the Tom Hanks, Steven Spielberg, Gary Goetzman miniseries *The Pacific*.

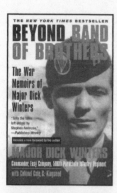

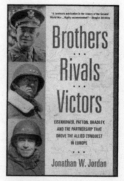
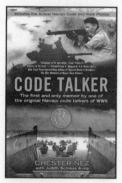

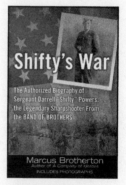

T192.0112